PENGUIN BOOKS

IN ORDER TO LIVE

Yeonmi Park was born in Hyesan, North Korea, in 1993. She lives in New York City and is a student at Columbia University.

In Order to Live

A North Korean Girl's Journey to Freedom

YEONMI PARK

with Maryanne Vollers

PENGUIN BOOKS

PENGUIN BOOKS

An imprint of Penguin Random House LLC
375 Hudson Street
New York, New York 10014
penguin.com

First published in the United States of America by Penguin Press,
an imprint of Penguin Random House LLC, 2015
Published in Penguin Books 2016

Photographs courtesy of Yeonmi Park

Map illustration by John Gilkes

ISBN 9781594206795 (hc.)
ISBN 9780143109747 (pbk.)

Printed in the United States of America
18th Printing

Designed by Amanda Dewey

Penguin is committed to publishing works of quality and integrity. In that spirit,
we are proud to offer this book to our readers; however, the story, the experiences,
and the words are the author's alone.

For my family,
and for anyone, anywhere, struggling for freedom

We tell ourselves stories in order to live.

—*Joan Didion*

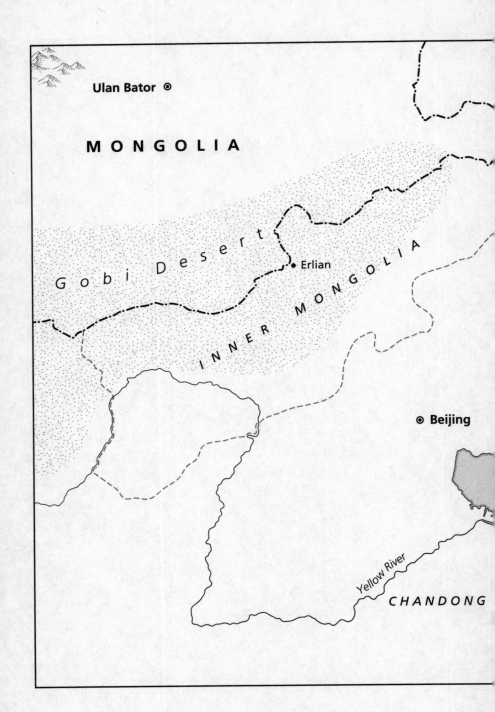

Contents

Prologue   *1*

PART ONE

North Korea

One Even the Birds and Mice Can Hear You Whisper   *9*

Two A Dangerous History   *20*

Three Swallows and Magpies   *29*

Four Tears of Blood   *37*

Five The Dear Leader   *45*

Six City of Dreams   *58*

Seven The Darkest Nights   *71*

Eight A Song for Chosun   *81*

Nine *Jangmadang* Generation   *92*

Ten The Lights of China   *105*

Eleven Missing   *115*

PART TWO

China

Twelve The Other Side of Darkness *125*

Thirteen A Deal with the Devil *139*

Fourteen A Birthday Gift *151*

Fifteen Dust and Bones *162*

Sixteen Kidnapped *169*

Seventeen Like Bread from the Sky *181*

Eighteen Following the Stars *187*

PART THREE

South Korea

Nineteen The Freedom Birds *201*

Twenty Dreams and Nightmares *213*

Twenty-one A Hungry Mind *223*

Twenty-two Now on *My Way to Meet You* *235*

Twenty-three Amazing Grace *245*

Twenty-four Homecoming *256*

Acknowledgments *269*

In Order to Live

Prologue

On the cold, black night of March 31, 2007, my mother and I scrambled down the steep, rocky bank of the frozen Yalu River that divides North Korea and China. There were patrols above us and below, and guard posts one hundred yards on either side of us manned by soldiers ready to shoot anyone attempting to cross the border. We had no idea what would come next, but we were desperate to get to China, where there might be a chance to survive.

I was thirteen years old and weighed only sixty pounds. Just a week earlier, I'd been in a hospital in my hometown of Hyesan along the Chinese border, suffering from a severe intestinal infection that the doctors had mistakenly diagnosed as appendicitis. I was still in terrible pain from the incision, and was so weak I could barely walk.

The young North Korean smuggler who was guiding us across the border insisted we had to go that night. He had paid some guards to look the other way, but he couldn't bribe all the soldiers in the area, so we had to be extremely cautious. I followed him in the darkness, but I was so unsteady that I had to scoot down the bank on my bottom, sending small avalanches of rocks crashing ahead of me. He turned and whispered angrily for me to stop making so much noise. But it was too late. We could see the silhouette of a North Korean soldier climbing up from the riverbed. If this was one of the bribed border guards, he didn't seem to recognize us.

"Go back!" the soldier shouted. "Get out of here!"

Our guide scrambled down to meet him and we could hear them talking in hushed voices. Our guide returned alone.

"Let's go," he said. "Hurry!"

It was early spring, and the weather was getting warmer, melting patches of the frozen river. The place where we crossed was steep and narrow, protected from the sun during the day so it was still solid enough to hold our weight—we hoped. Our guide made a cell phone call to someone on the other side, the Chinese side, and then whispered, "Run!"

The guide started running, but my feet would not move and I clung to my mother. I was so scared that I was completely paralyzed. The guide ran back for us, grabbed my hands, and dragged me across the ice. When we reached solid ground, we started running and didn't stop until we were out of sight of the border guards.

The riverbank was dark, but the lights of Chaingbai, China, glowed just ahead of us. I turned to take a quick glance back at the place where I was born. The electric power grid was down, as usual, and all I could see was a black, lifeless horizon. I felt my heart pounding out of my chest as we arrived at a small shack on the edge of some flat, vacant fields.

I wasn't dreaming of freedom when I escaped from North Korea. I didn't even know what it meant to be free. All I knew was that if my family stayed behind, we would probably die—from starvation, from disease, from the inhuman conditions of a prison labor camp. The hunger had become unbearable; I was willing to risk my life for the promise of a bowl of rice.

But there was more to our journey than our own survival. My mother and I were searching for my older sister, Eunmi, who had left for China a few days earlier and had not been heard from since. We hoped that she would be there waiting for us when we crossed the river. Instead the only person to greet us was a bald, middle-aged Chinese man, an ethnic North Korean like many of the people living in this border area. The man said something to my mother, and then led her around the side of the building. From where I waited I could hear my mother pleading, *"Aniyo! Aniyo!"* No! No!

I knew then that something was terribly wrong. We had come to a bad place, maybe even worse than the one we had left.

I am most grateful for two things: that I was born in North Korea, and that I escaped from North Korea. Both of these events shaped me, and I would not trade them for an ordinary and peaceful life. But there is more to the story of how I became who I am today.

Like tens of thousands of other North Koreans, I escaped my homeland and settled in South Korea, where we are still considered citizens, as if a sealed border and nearly seventy years of conflict and tension never divided us. North and South Koreans have the same ethnic backgrounds, and we speak the same language—except in the North there are no words for things like "shopping malls," "liberty," or even "love," at least as the rest of the world knows it. The only true "love" we can express is worship for the Kims, a dynasty of dictators who have ruled North Korea for three generations. The regime blocks all outside information, all videos and movies, and jams radio signals. There is no World Wide Web and no Wikipedia. The only books are filled with propaganda telling us that we live in the greatest country in the world, even though at least half of North Koreans live in extreme poverty and many are chronically malnourished. My former country doesn't even call itself North Korea—it claims to be Chosun, the true Korea, a perfect socialist paradise where 25 million people live only to serve the Supreme Leader, Kim Jong Un. Many of us who have escaped call ourselves "defectors" because by refusing to accept our fate and die for the Leader, we have deserted our duty. The regime calls us traitors. If I tried to return, I would be executed.

The information blockade works both ways: not only does the government attempt to keep all foreign media from reaching its people, it also prevents outsiders from learning the truth about North Korea. The regime is known as the Hermit Kingdom because it tries to make itself unknowable. Only those of us who have escaped can describe what really goes on behind the sealed borders. But until recently, our stories were seldom heard.

I arrived in South Korea in the spring of 2009, a fifteen-year-old with no money and the equivalent of two years of primary school. Five years later, I was a sophomore at a top university in Seoul, a police administration major with a growing awareness of the burning need for justice in the land where I was born.

I have told the story of my escape from North Korea many times, in many forums. I have described how human traffickers tricked my mother and me into following them to China, where my mother protected me and sacrificed herself to be raped by the broker who had targeted me. Once in China, we continued to look for my sister, without success. My father crossed the border to join us in our search, but he died of untreated cancer a few months later. In 2009, my mother and I were rescued by Christian missionaries, who led us to the Mongolian border with China. From there we walked through the frigid Gobi Desert one endless winter night, following the stars to freedom.

All this is true, but it is not the whole story.

Before now, only my mother knew what really happened in the two years that passed between the night we crossed the Yalu River into China and the day we arrived in South Korea to begin a new life. I told almost nothing of my story to the other defectors and human rights advocates I met in South Korea. I believed that, somehow, if I refused to acknowledge the unspeakable past, it would disappear. I convinced myself that a lot of it never happened; I taught myself to forget the rest.

But as I began to write this book, I realized that without the whole truth my life would have no power, no real meaning. With the help of my mother, the memories of our lives in North Korea and China came back to me like scenes from a forgotten nightmare. Some of the images reappeared with a terrible clarity; others were hazy, or scrambled like a deck of cards spilled on the floor. The process of writing has been the process of remembering, and of trying to make sense out of those memories.

Along with writing, reading has helped me order my world. As soon as I arrived in South Korea and could get my hands on translations of the world's great books, I began devouring them. Later I was able to read them in English. And as I began to write my own book, I came across a famous line by Joan Didion, "We tell ourselves stories in order to live." Even though the writer and I come from such different cultures, I feel the truth of those words echoing inside me. I understand that sometimes the only way we can survive our own memories is to shape them into a story that makes sense out of events that seem inexplicable.

Along my journey I have seen the horrors that humans can inflict on one another, but I've also witnessed acts of tenderness and kindness and sacrifice in the worst imaginable circumstances. I know that it is possible to lose part of your humanity in order to survive. But I also know that the spark of human dignity is never completely extinguished, and that given the oxygen of freedom and the power of love, it can grow again.

This is my story of the choices I made in order to live.

PART ONE

North Korea

One

Even the Birds and Mice Can Hear You Whisper

The Yalu River winds like the tail of a dragon between China and North Korea on its way to the Yellow Sea. At Hyesan it opens into a valley in the Paektu Mountains, where the city of 200,000 sprawls between rolling hills and a high plateau covered with fields, patches of trees, and graves. The river, usually shallow and tame, is frozen solid during winter, which lasts the better part of the year. This is the coldest part of North Korea, with temperatures sometimes plunging to minus-40 degrees Fahrenheit. Only the toughest survive.

To me, Hyesan was home.

Just across the river is the Chinese city of Chaingbai, which has a large population of ethnic Koreans. Families on both sides of the border have been trading with one another for generations. As a child I would often stand in the darkness and stare across the river at the lights of Chaingbai, wondering what was going on beyond my city's limits. It was exciting to watch the colorful fireworks explode in the velvet black sky during festivals and Chinese New Year. We never had such things on our side of the border. Sometimes, when I walked down to the river to fill my buckets with water and the damp wind was blowing just right, I could actually smell delicious food, oily noodles and dumplings cooking in the kitchens on the other side. The same wind carried the voices of the Chinese children who were playing on the opposite bank.

"Hey, you! Are you hungry over there?" the boys shouted in Korean.

"No! Shut up, you fat Chinese!" I shouted back.

This wasn't true. In fact, I was very hungry, but there was no use in talking about it.

I came into this world too soon. My mother was only seven months pregnant when she went into labor, and when I was born on October 4, 1993, I weighed less than three pounds. The doctor at the hospital in Hyesan told my mother that I was so small there wasn't anything they could do for me. "She might live or she might die," he said. "We don't know." It was up to me to live.

No matter how many blankets my mother wrapped around me, she couldn't keep me warm. So she heated up a stone and put it in the blanket with me, and that's how I survived. A few days later, my parents brought me home, and waited.

My sister, Eunmi, had been born two years earlier, and this time my father, Park Jin Sik, was hoping for a son. In patriarchal North Korea, it was the male line that really mattered. However, he quickly recovered from his disappointment. Most of the time it's the mother who makes the strongest bond with a baby, but my father was the one who could soothe me when I was crying. It was in my father's arms that I felt protected and cherished. Both my mother and my father encouraged me, from the start, to be proud of who I am.

W hen I was very young, we lived in a one-story house perched on a hill above the railroad tracks that curved like a rusty spine through the city.

Our house was small and drafty, and because we shared a wall with a neighbor we could always hear what was going on next door. We could also hear mice squeaking and skittering around in the ceiling at night. But it was paradise to me because we were there together as a family.

My first memories are of the dark and the cold. During the winter months, the most popular place in our house was a small fireplace that burned wood or coal or whatever we could find. We cooked on top of the fire, and there were channels running under the cement floor to carry the smoke to a wooden chimney on the other side of the house. This traditional heating system was supposed to keep the room warm, but it was no match for the icy nights. At the end of the day, my mother would spread a thick blanket out next to the fire and we would all climb under the covers—first my mother, then me, then my sister, and my father on the end, in the coldest spot. Once the sun went down, you couldn't see anything at all. In our part of North Korea, it was normal to go for weeks and even months without any electricity, and candles were very expensive. So we played games in the dark. Sometimes under the covers we would tease each other.

"Whose foot is this?" my mother would say, poking with her toe.

"It's mine, it's mine!" Eunmi would cry.

On winter evenings and mornings, and even in summertime, everywhere we looked we could see smoke coming from the chimneys of Hyesan. Our neighborhood was very cozy and small, and we knew everyone who lived there. If smoke was not coming out of someone's house, we'd go knock on the door to check if everything was okay.

The unpaved lanes between houses were too narrow for cars, although this wasn't much of a problem because there were so few cars. People in our neighborhood got around on foot, or for the few who could afford one, on bicycle or motorbike. The paths would turn slippery with mud after a rain, and that was the best time for the neighborhood kids to play our favorite chasing game. But I was smaller and slower than the other children my age and always had a hard time fitting in and keeping up.

When I started school, Eunmi sometimes had to fight the older kids to defend me. She wasn't very big, either, but she was smart and quick. She was my protector and playmate. When it snowed, she carried me up the hills around our neighborhood, put me in her lap, and wrapped her arms around me. I held on tight as we slid back down on our bottoms, screaming and laughing. I was just happy to be part of her world.

In the summer, all the kids went down to play in the Yalu River, but I never learned how to swim. I just sat on the bank while the others paddled out into the current. Sometimes my sister or my best friend, Yong Ja, would see me by myself and bring me some pretty rocks they'd found in the deep river. And sometimes they held me in their arms and carried me a little way into the water before bringing me back to shore.

Yong Ja and I were the same age, and we lived in the same part of town. I liked her because we were both good at using our imaginations to create our own toys. You could find a few manufactured dolls and other toys in the market, but they were usually too expensive. Instead we made little bowls and animals out of mud, and sometimes even miniature tanks; homemade military toys were very big in North

Korea. But we girls were obsessed with paper dolls and spent hours cutting them out of thick paper, making dresses and scarves for them out of scraps.

Sometimes my mother made pinwheels for us, and we would fasten them on to the metal footbridge above the railroad we called the Cloud Bridge. Years later, when life was much harder and more complicated, I would pass by that bridge and think of how happy it made us to watch those pinwheels spin in the open breeze.

When I was young, I didn't hear the background noise of mechanical sounds like I do now in South Korea and the United States. There weren't garbage trucks churning, horns honking, or phones ringing everywhere. All I could hear were the sounds people were making: women washing dishes, mothers calling their children, the clink of spoons and chopsticks on rice bowls as families sat down to eat. Sometimes I could hear my friends being scolded by their parents. There was no music blaring in the background, no eyes glued to smartphones back then. But there was human intimacy and connection, something that is hard to find in the modern world I inhabit today.

At our house in Hyesan, our water pipes were almost always dry, so my mother usually carried our clothes down to the river and washed them there. When she brought them back, she put them on the warm floor to dry.

Because electricity was so rare in our neighborhood, whenever the lights came on people were so happy they would sing and clap and shout. Even in the middle of the night, we would wake up to celebrate. When you have so little, just the smallest thing can make you happy—and that is one of the very few features of life in North Korea that I actually miss. Of course, the lights would never stay on for long. When they flickered off, we just said, "Oh, well," and went back to sleep.

Even when the electricity came on the power was very low, so many families had a voltage booster to help run the appliances. These machines were always catching on fire, and one March night it happened at our house while my parents were out. I was just a baby, and all I remember is waking up and crying while someone carried me through the smoke and flames. I don't know if it was my sister or our neighbor who saved me. My mother came running when someone told her about the blaze, but my sister and I were both already safe in the neighbor's house. Our home was destroyed by the fire, but right away my father rebuilt it with his own hands.

After that, we planted a garden in our small fenced yard. My mother and sister weren't interested in gardening, but my father and I loved it. We put in squash and cabbage and cucumbers and sunflowers. My father also planted beautiful fuchsia flowers we called "ear drops" along the fence. I adored draping the long delicate blossoms from my ears and pretending they were earrings. My mother asked my father why he was wasting valuable space planting flowers, but he ignored her.

In North Korea, people lived close to nature, and they developed skills to predict the next day's weather. We didn't have the Internet and usually couldn't watch the government's broadcast on television because of the electricity shortage. So we had to figure it out ourselves.

During the long summer nights, our neighbors would all sit around outside their houses in the evening air. There were no chairs; we just sat on the ground, looking at the sky. If we saw millions of stars up there, someone would remark, "Tomorrow will be a sunny day." And we'd all murmur agreement. If there were only thousands of stars, someone else might say, "Looks like tomorrow will be cloudy." That was our local forecast.

The best day of every month was Noodle Day, when my mother bought fresh, moist noodles that were made in a machine in town. We wanted them to last a long time, so we spread them out on the warm kitchen floor to dry. It was like a holiday for my sister and me because we would get to sneak a few noodles and eat them while they were still soft and sweet. In the earliest years of my life, before the worst of the famine that struck North Korea in the mid-1990s had gripped our city, our friends would come around and we would share the noodles with them. In North Korea, you are supposed to share everything. But later, when times were much harder for our family and for the country, my mother told us to chase the children away. We couldn't afford to share anything.

During the good times, a family meal would consist of rice, kim-chi, some kind of beans, and seaweed soup. But those things were too expensive to eat during the lean times. Sometimes we would skip meals, and often all we had to eat was a thin porridge of wheat or barley, beans, or black frozen potatoes ground and made into cakes filled with cabbage.

The country I grew up in was not like the one my parents had known as children in the 1960s and 1970s. When they were young, the state took care of everyone's basic needs: clothes, medical care, food. After the Cold War ended, the Communist countries that had been propping up the North Korean regime all but abandoned it, and our state-controlled economy collapsed. North Koreans were suddenly on their own.

I was too young to realize how desperate things were becoming in the grown-up world, as my family tried to adapt to the massive changes in North Korea during the 1990s. After my sister and I were asleep, my parents would sometimes lie awake, sick with worry, wondering what they could do to keep us all from starving to death.

Anything I did overhear, I learned quickly not to repeat. I was taught never to express my opinion, never to question anything. I was taught to simply follow what the government told me to do or say or think. I actually believed that our Dear Leader, Kim Jong Il, could read my mind, and I would be punished for my bad thoughts. And if he didn't hear me, spies were everywhere, listening at the windows and watching in the school yard. We all belonged to *inminban*, or neighborhood "people's units," and we were ordered to inform on anyone who said the wrong thing. We lived in fear, and almost everyone—my mother included—had a personal experience that demonstrated the dangers of talking.

I was only nine months old when Kim Il Sung died on July 8, 1994. North Koreans worshipped the eighty-two-year-old "Great Leader." At the time of his death, Kim Il Sung had ruled North Korea with an iron grip for almost five decades, and true believers—my mother included—thought that Kim Il Sung was actually immortal. His passing was a time of passionate mourning, and also uncertainty in the country. The Great Leader's son, Kim Jong Il, had already been chosen to succeed his father, but the huge void Kim Il Sung left behind had everyone on edge.

My mother strapped me on her back to join the thousands of mourners who daily flocked to the plaza-like Kim Il Sung monument in Hyesan to weep and wail for the fallen Leader during the official mourning period. The mourners left offerings of flowers and cups of rice liquor to show their adoration and grief.

During that time, one of my father's relatives was visiting from northeast China, where many ethnic North Koreans lived. Because he was a foreigner, he was not as reverent about the Great Leader, and when my mother came back from one of her trips to the monument, Uncle Yong Soo repeated a story he had just heard. The Pyongyang government had announced that Kim Il Sung had died of a heart attack, but Yong Soo reported that a Chinese friend told him he had heard from a North Korean police officer that it wasn't true. The real cause of death, he said, was *hwa-byung*—a common diagnosis in both North and South Korea that roughly translates into "disease caused by mental or emotional stress." Yong Soo had heard that there were disagreements between Kim Il Sung and Kim Jong Il over the elder Kim's plans to hold talks with South Korea. . . .

"Stop!" my mother said. "Don't say another word!" She was so upset that Yong Soo would dare to spread rumors about the regime that she had to be rude to her guest and shut him up.

The next day she and her best friend were visiting the monument to place more flowers when they noticed someone had vandalized the offerings.

"Oh, there are such bad people in this world!" her friend said.

"You are so right!" my mother said. "You wouldn't believe the evil rumor that our enemies have been spreading." And then she told her friend about the lies she had heard.

The following day she was walking across the Cloud Bridge when she noticed an official-looking car parked in the lane below our house, and a large group of men gathered around it. She immediately knew something awful was about to happen.

The visitors were plainclothes agents of the dreaded *bo-wi-bu*, or National Security Agency, that ran the political prison camps and investigated threats to the regime. Everybody knew these men could take you away and you would never be heard from again. Worse, these weren't locals; they had been sent from headquarters.

The senior agent met my mother at our door and led her to our neighbor's house, which he had borrowed for the afternoon. They both sat, and he looked at her with eyes like black glass.

"Do you know why I'm here?" he asked.

"Yes, I do," she said.

"So where did you hear that?" he said.

She told him she'd heard the rumor from her husband's Chinese uncle, who had heard it from a friend.

"What do you think of it?" he said.

"It's a terrible, evil rumor!" she said, most sincerely. "It's a lie told by our enemies who are trying to destroy the greatest nation in the world!"

"What do you think you have done wrong?" he said, flatly.

"Sir, I should have gone to the party organization to report it. I was wrong to just tell it to an individual."

"No, you are wrong," he said. "You should never have let those words out of your mouth."

Now she was sure she was going to die. She kept telling him she was sorry, begging to spare her life for the sake of her two babies. As we say in Korea, she begged until she thought her hands would wear off.

Finally, he said in a sharp voice that chilled her bones, "You must never mention this again. Not to your friends or your husband or your children. Do you understand what will happen if you do?"

She did. Completely.

Next he interrogated Uncle Yong Soo, who was nervously waiting with the family at our house. My mother thinks that she was spared any punishment because Yong Soo confirmed to the agent how angry she had been when he told her the rumor.

When it was over, the agents rode away in their car. My uncle went back to China. When my father asked my mother what the secret police wanted from her, she said it was nothing she could talk about, and never mentioned it again. My father went to his grave without knowing how close they had come to disaster.

Many years later, after she told me her story, I finally understood why when my mother sent me off to school she never said, "Have a good day," or even, "Watch out for strangers." What she always said was, "Take care of your mouth."

In most countries, a mother encourages her children to ask about everything, but not in North Korea. As soon as I was old enough to understand, my mother warned me that I should be careful about what I was saying. "Remember, Yeonmi-ya," she said gently, "even when you think you're alone, the birds and mice can hear you whisper." She didn't mean to scare me, but I felt a deep darkness and horror inside me.

Two

A Dangerous History

I think my father would have become a millionaire if he had grown up in South Korea or the United States. But he was born in North Korea, where family connections and party loyalty are all that matter, and hard work guarantees you nothing but more hard work and a constant struggle to survive.

Park Jin Sik was born in the industrial port city of Hamhung on March 4, 1962, into a military family with good political connections. This should have given him a great advantage in life, because in North Korea all of your opportunities are determined by your caste, or *songbun*. When Kim Il Sung came to power after World War II, he upended the traditional feudal system that divided the people into landlords and peasants, nobility and commoners, priests and scholars. He ordered background checks on every citizen to find out everything about them and their families, going back generations. In the *songbun* system, everyone is ranked among three main groups, based on their supposed loyalty to the regime.

The highest is the "core" class made up of honored revolutionaries—peasants, veterans, or relatives of those who fought or died for
the North—and those who have demonstrated great loyalty to the
Kim family and are part of the apparatus that keeps them in power.
Second is the "basic" or "wavering" class, made up of those who once
lived in the South or had family there, former merchants, intellectu-
als, or any ordinary person who might not be trusted to have complete loyalty to the new order. Finally, lowest of all, is the "hostile"
class, including former landowners and their descendants, capitalists,
former South Korean soldiers, Christians or other religious followers,
the families of political prisoners, and any other perceived enemies of
the state.

It is extremely difficult to move to a higher *songbun*, but it is
very easy to be cast down into the lowest levels through no fault of
your own. And as my father and his family found out, once you lose
your *songbun* status, you lose everything else you have achieved
along with it.

My father's father, Park Chang Gyu, grew up in the countryside
near Hyesan when Korea was a Japanese colony.

For more than four thousand years there has been one Korean
people, but many different Koreas. Legend tells us that our history
began in 2333 B.C., with a kingdom called Chosun, which means
"Morning Land." Despite its soothing name, my homeland has rarely
been peaceful. The Korean peninsula lay at the crossroads of great
empires, and over the centuries Korean kingdoms had to fight off
invaders from Manchuria to Mongolia and beyond. Then, in the early
twentieth century, the expanding Japanese empire slowly absorbed
Korea using threats and treaties, finally annexing the whole country
in 1910. That was two years before the birth of North Korea's first

Leader, Kim Il Sung, and eleven years before my grandfather Park was born.

The Japanese were despotic colonial rulers who tried to destroy Korean culture and turn us into second-class citizens in our own land. They outlawed the Korean language and took over our farms and industries. This behavior sparked a nationalist resistance to Japanese rule that was met with violent suppression. Like many Koreans, Kim Il Sung's parents moved the family across the northern border to Manchuria, then a part of the Chinese empire. After the Japanese invaded Manchuria in the early 1930s, our future Great Leader joined a guerrilla group fighting the Japanese occupiers. But at the outset of World War II, Kim Il Sung joined the Soviet army and (as I later learned), contrary to North Korean propaganda, which has him almost singlehandedly defeating the Japanese—spent the war at a military base far from the fighting.

When I was growing up, we didn't talk about what our families did during those times. In North Korea, any history can be dangerous. What I know about my father's side of the family comes from the few stories my father told my mother.

At the start of World War II, Grandfather Park was working for Japanese managers in the finance department of Hyesan's administrative office, or city hall. It was there that he met his future wife, Jung Hye Soon, who was also working at the city hall. She was an orphan who had been raised by her aunt, and she'd had a very hard life before she met my grandfather. Their courtship was unusual, because unlike so many Korean couples whose marriages are arranged by their parents, my grandparents actually knew and liked each other before their wedding.

My grandfather kept his civil service job all through World War II. After the Japanese surrendered on August 15, 1945, the Soviet army swept into the northern part of Korea, while the American military took charge of the South—and this set the stage for the agony my country has endured for more than seventy years. An arbitrary line was drawn along the 38th parallel, dividing the peninsula into two administrative zones: North and South Korea. The United States flew an anti-Communist exile named Syngman Rhee into Seoul and ushered him into power as the first president of the Republic of Korea. In the North, Kim Il Sung, who had by then become a Soviet major, was installed as leader of the Democratic People's Republic of Korea, or DPRK.

The Soviets quickly rounded up all eligible men to establish a North Korean military force. My grandfather was taken from his job at city hall and turned into an officer in the People's Army.

By 1949, both the United States and the Soviet Union had withdrawn their troops and turned the peninsula over to the new puppet leaders. It did not go well. Kim Il Sung was a Stalinist and an ultranationalist dictator who decided to reunify the country in the summer of 1950 by invading the South with Russian tanks and thousands of troops. In North Korea, we were taught that the Yankee imperialists started the war, and our soldiers gallantly fought off their evil invasion. In fact, the United States military returned to Korea for the express purpose of *defending* the South—bolstered by an official United Nations force—and quickly drove Kim Il Sung's army all the way to the Yalu River, nearly taking over the country. They were stopped only when Chinese soldiers surged across the border and fought the Americans back to the 38th parallel. By the end of this senseless war, at least three million Koreans had been killed or wounded, millions were refugees, and most of the country was in ruins.

In 1953, both sides agreed to end the fighting, but they never signed a peace treaty. To this day we are still officially at war, and both the governments of the North and South believe that they are the legitimate representatives of all Koreans.

. . .

Grandfather Park was a financial officer and never fired a shot during the Korean War. After the armistice, he remained in the military, traveling with his family from post to post. He was based in Hamhung, about 180 miles south of Hyesan, when my father was born—the fourth of five children and the youngest son. Later, when my grandfather retired from active duty, the government resettled him and his family in Hyesan. My grandfather's position as an officer and a member of the ruling Workers' Party of Korea gave him good *songbun* status, and he was awarded another job as finance manager at the commissary that supplied goods to military families. At least for a while, the family prospered along with North Korea's growing economy.

During the 1950s and 1960s, China and the Soviet Union poured money into North Korea to help it rebuild. The North has coal and minerals in its mountains, and it was always the richer, more industrialized part of the country. It bounced back more quickly than the South, which was still mostly agricultural and slow to recover from the war. But that started to change in the 1970s and 1980s, as South Korea became a manufacturing center and North Korea's Soviet-style system began to collapse under its own weight. The economy was centrally planned and completely controlled by the state. There was no private property—at least officially—and all the farms were collectivized, although people could grow some vegetables to sell in small, highly controlled markets. The government provided all jobs, paid everyone's salary, and distributed rations for most food and consumer goods.

While my parents were growing up, the distribution system was still subsidized by the Soviet Union and China, so few people were starving, but nobody outside the elite really prospered. At the same

DANGEROUS HISTORY25

time, supply wasn't meeting demand for the kinds of items people wanted, like imported clothing, electronics, and special foods. While the favored classes had access to many of these goods through government-run department stores, the prices were usually too high for most people to afford. Any ordinary citizen who fancied foreign cigarettes or alcohol or Japanese-made handbags would have to buy them on the black market. The usual route for those goods was from the north, through China.

My father went into the military sometime around 1980, when he was in his late teens. Like most North Korean men from the middle and upper classes, he was conscripted for ten years of service, although with connections that could be reduced to as little as two. But less than a year after my father joined the army, he got very sick with a burst appendix. After four or five surgeries to control complications from the infection, his military service was over for good. This could have been a catastrophe for him, because North Korean men without military backgrounds are usually shut out of the best jobs. But when he returned to Hyesan with nothing to do, his father suggested he study finance. He was able to enroll in a three-year program at the Hyesan Economic College. The rest of the family was also doing well. My father's older brother Park Jin was attending medical school in Hyesan, and his eldest brother, Park Dong Il, was a middle school teacher in Hamhung. His older sister had married and moved to Pyongyang where she worked as a waitress, and his little sister was attending school in Hyesan.

But disaster struck in 1980 when Dong Il was accused of raping one of his students and attempting to kill his wife. I never learned all the details of what happened, or even if the charges were true, but he ended up being sentenced to twenty years of hard labor. It was only because of Grandfather Park's connections that he escaped execution. It is common for nonpolitical prisoners to be released from prison before they die, to save the government the trouble of sending their bodies home. So after serving twelve years, Dong Il was let out on sick leave and he returned to Hyesan. Nobody in the family ever spoke about his past. I remember him as a frail and quiet man who was always kind to me. He died when I was still a little girl.

In North Korea, if one member of the family commits a serious crime, everybody is considered a criminal. Suddenly my father's family lost its favorable social and political status.

There are more than fifty subgroups within the main *songbun* castes, and once you become an adult, your status is constantly being monitored and adjusted by the authorities. A network of casual neighborhood informants and official police surveillance ensures that nothing you do or your family does goes unnoticed. Everything about you is recorded and stored in local administrative offices and in big national organizations, and the information is used to determine where you can live, where you can go to school, and where you can work. With a superior *songbun,* you can join the Workers' Party, which gives you access to political power. You can go to a good university and get a good job. With a poor one, you can end up on a collective farm chopping rice paddies for the rest of your life. And, in times of famine, starving to death.

All of Grandfather Park's connections could not save his career after his eldest son was convicted of attempted murder. He was fired from his job at the commissary shortly after Dong Il was sent to prison, although no official reason was given for his dismissal. Fortunately, his younger sons were less affected by the scandal and managed to complete their educations. My uncle Park Jin finished medical school and became a professor at Hyesan Medical University and later became administrator at the medical college. He was an excellent student and clever political player who managed to succeed despite his family's problems. My father earned his degree in economic planning and, like his father before him, was hired to work in the finance office in Hyesan's city hall. But after only a year, there was a restructuring in the administrative offices and he lost his job. His poor *songbun* had finally caught up with him.

My father realized he would have no future unless he found a way to join the Workers' Party. He decided to become a laborer at a local metal foundry where he could work hard and prove his loyalty to the regime. He was able to build good relationships with the people who had power at his workplace, including the party representative there. Before long, he had his membership.

By that time, my father had also started a side business to make some extra money. This was a bold move, because any business venture outside of state control was illegal. But my father was unusual in that he had a natural entrepreneurial spirit and what some might call a healthy contempt for rules. He also had the luck to be living at the right time and in the right part of the country to turn his business into a big success. At least for a while.

Hyesan already had a long-established tradition of cross-border trade with China and a small but lively black market for everything from dried fish to electronics. During the 1980s, women were allowed to sell food and handicrafts in makeshift markets, but general trading was still an underground and specialized activity. My father joined a small but growing class of black market operators who found ways to exploit cracks in the state-controlled economy. He started small. My father discovered that he could buy a carton of top-quality cigarettes for 70 to 100 won on the black market in Hyesan, then sell *each* cigarette for 7 to 10 won in the North Korean interior. At that time, a kilogram—2.2 pounds—of rice cost around 25 won, so cigarettes were obviously very valuable.

The government had placed more restrictions on travel in North Korea, and there was a lot of paperwork involved in traveling out of town. First my father needed permission to leave the factory where he worked. He would negotiate a fee with a doctor to write him a note saying he was sick, then he would tell his supervisor that he needed to go out of town for a few days for treatment. The supervisor would issue him papers. Then my father would go to the police and bribe them for a travel permit.

My father traveled by train to small cities where there weren't big black markets. He hid the cigarettes in his bags, all over his body, and in every pocket. He had to keep moving to avoid being searched by the police, who were always looking for contraband. Sometimes the police discovered him and confiscated the cigarettes or threatened to hit him with a metal stick if he didn't turn over his money. My father had to convince the police that it was in everybody's interest to let him make a profit so that he could keep coming back and giving them cigarettes as bribes. Often they agreed. He was a born salesman.

Although I know he would have preferred a safer and more conventional life as a high government official, that was never to be his fate. Almost anywhere else, business would have been my father's vocation. But in North Korea, it was simply a means to survive. And it made him an outlaw.

Three

Swallows and Magpies

M y father's business began with cigarettes and soon grew to include Chinese-made clothes, a product in high demand. In the summer of 1989, he traveled to Kowon, a small city near North Korea's east coast, to sell his goods, and while in town stopped to visit with his friend Byeon Min Sik, another ambitious young man whom my father had known in Hyesan. It was there that my father met his friend's younger sister, Keum Sook. My mother.

She was four years younger than my father, and her *songbun* status was just as poor as his, also through no fault of her own. While my father had to struggle because his brother was in prison, she was considered untrustworthy because her paternal grandfather had owned land when Korea was a Japanese colony. The stigma passed down through three generations, and when my mother was born in 1966, she was already considered a member of the "hostile" class and barred from the privileges of the elite.

My mother's father, Byeon Ung Rook, came from North Hamgyong province in the northernmost part of Korea. His family wasn't very wealthy, but they owned just enough property to be considered landlords. By the time my grandfather Byeon was born in 1931, the family had already lost their money. That was the same year that Japan decided to expand its empire by invading and occupying the three Chinese provinces that make up Manchuria, just north of the Korean border.

Hundreds of thousands of ethnic Koreans had already settled in Manchuria, and the border was notoriously porous. When Japan occupied both regions during the 1930s and 1940s, it was even easier to travel back and forth.

In 1933, when my grandfather Byeon was two years old, the whole family moved to Hunchun, China, just across the Tumen River from Hamgyong. When World War II broke out, he was still a schoolboy, but he ended up in the fighting. My mother never knew which army he belonged to, because my grandfather never spoke of it.

After the war ended, he remained in China but often visited his North Korean homeland. When he was twenty-two years old, right before the Korean War began in 1950, he made a visit to Onsong, a border town where his father had once owned property. There he met a group of men who were on their way to the Soviet Union to work as loggers. He joined them for dinner, and they kept buying rounds of drinks. Finally, he left them to walk back alone to the inn where he was staying, but he was so drunk that he lay down on the railroad tracks and fell asleep. My grandfather woke up the next day in an Onsong hospital with an arm and a leg missing and no idea how he got there. He was told that a train had run over him while he slept, and he'd survived only because a railroad monitor found him and brought him to a doctor.

Grandfather Byeon remained in North Korea to heal. His arm was completely gone, but enough of his leg remained that he was fitted with a prosthetic limb and learned to walk without crutches. By the time he recovered, the Korean War was ending. In fact, the devastating injury might have saved his life, because he would almost certainly have ended up fighting in a conflict that claimed more than three million lives.

The United States dropped more bombs on North Korea than it had during the entire Pacific campaign in World War II. The Americans bombed every city and village, and they kept bombing until there were no major buildings left to destroy. Then they bombed the dams to flood the crops. The damage was unimaginable, and nobody knows how many civilians were killed and maimed.

After the war, the North Korean government set up nursing centers for the disabled who had no families to care for them. One of these facilities in Onsong was where Grandfather met his future wife, Hwang Ok Soon. She was an orphan from a rural community in what was now South Korea, and her father had been a resistance fighter against Japan during Korea's colonial days. When she was ten years old, he was arrested and never heard from again. After that, Grandmother Hwang was abandoned by her family, and ended up working as a farm laborer in Tumen, China—which was then part of the Japanese empire.

She returned to her home country after the Japanese surrendered and Korea gained independence. Unfortunately, she was living in the Communist North when Korea was partitioned. In 1952, she was working at a munitions factory in the port city of Chongjin on the East Sea when her leg was injured in a bombing raid and had to be amputated.

She was sent to a nursing facility to recover and learn to use her wooden leg. She was still young and single, but it was not likely that an able-bodied person would marry someone with a disability. So her best hope was to find a husband with a similar condition. My grandfather Byeon apparently had the same idea, and he was visiting nursing homes all over the northern provinces, looking for a bride. The way she told the story, my grandmother saw him walking around the hallways and took pity on him. "This man is in bad shape," she thought. "If I don't marry him, he'll never find a wife."

They were wed shortly after the war ended, and she traveled the 150 miles north with him, across the Chinese border to his home in Hunchun. By 1956, my grandmother was pregnant with their first child, my mother's older sister. She was also miserable and homesick. Even though she had spent time in China, she never learned to speak Chinese. And she had a terrible craving for seafood, especially octopus the way it is prepared in Cheongjin. Finally, she couldn't stand it anymore, and she left her husband behind while she went to find some octopus to eat. She could be an extremely emotional woman, and very strong-willed. When she made up her mind to do something, she could not be dissuaded. My grandfather had no choice but to follow her.

Cheongjin was once a small fishing village, but the Japanese had turned it into an industrial port, and the North Korean government was rebuilding it as a major manufacturing and military center. My grandparents agreed that it was no place to raise a family. They were both loyal followers of Kim Il Sung, and they worried about the capitalistic tendencies in the border areas. They didn't want their children to be tempted by smuggling and other criminal activities.

They traveled south by rail to find a place to settle deep in the countryside. This was how my mother's family came to live in Kowon, a small city near a big agricultural river delta backed by rolling mountains. There were rice paddies and orchards, and none of the corrupting influences of the bustling border towns. It should have been a fresh start, but they came to Kowon at the time that Kim Il Sung began purging North Korea of class traitors. All citizens had to be investigated to determine their loyalty and record their *songbun*. Unfortunately, my grandfather was very truthful, and he told the investigator that his father was a landowner from Onsong. From then on he was cursed with a bad *songbun*, and there was no chance for him to join the party and get ahead in life. He was assigned a job in a button factory.

My mother's older sister was born in Kowon in 1957, followed by three more children—two boys and then my mother, the youngest, who was born on July 16, 1966. They all grew up to be loyal followers of the regime, like their parents.

My mother was an excellent student and a gifted singer and musician who accompanied herself on the accordion and guitar. In North Korean propaganda videos, you often see beautiful women dressed in traditional *hanbok*—the colorful jackets and high-waisted skirts that make them look like floating flowers—who sing such high and mournful songs that the audience bursts into tears. That's what my mother did so well.

When she was young, she wanted to perform professionally, but her teachers told her she had to study to go to university. Her father also discouraged a career as a performer. Instead she concentrated on her studies and memorized poetry praising the Great Leader and his son, Kim Jong Il, his chosen heir.

It was unusual for a North Korean woman of her status to get a higher education. But my mother was such a good scholar that she was accepted at a college in the nearby city of Hamhung. If given a choice, she would have liked to have become a doctor. But only students from better families are allowed a say in what they will study. The school administration decided she would major in inorganic chemistry, and that's what she did. When she graduated, party officials sent her back to Kowon to work in a chemical factory there. She was assigned a low-level job making the ingredients for fragrances to put in soap and toothpaste. A few months later, she was allowed to switch to a better job at another factory that made clothes for export to the Soviet Union.

Despite what others might call disappointments, she never questioned the regime's authority to control her life. Unlike North Koreans who grew up along the borders, my mother had no exposure to the outside world or foreign ideas. She knew only what the regime taught her and she remained a proud and pure revolutionary. And because she had a poet's heart, she felt an enormous emotional connection to the official propaganda. She sincerely believed that North Korea was the center of the universe and that Kim Il Sung and Kim Jong Il had supernatural powers. She believed that Kim Il Sung caused the sun to rise and that when Kim Jong Il was born in a cabin on our sacred Mount Paektu (he was actually born in Russia), his arrival was marked by a double rainbow and a bright new star in the sky. She was so brainwashed that when Kim Il Sung died she started to panic. It was like God himself had died. "How can the Earth still spin on its axis?" she wondered. The laws of physics she had studied in college were overcome by the propaganda that was drilled into her all her life. It would be many years before she realized that Kim Il Sung and Kim Jong Il were just men who had learned from Joseph Stalin, their Soviet role model, how to make people worship them like gods.

My mother was still living at home and working in the clothing factory when she met my father in the summer of 1989. It had become my father's habit to stay with her brother Min Sik while he was conducting his black market business in Kowon. Since Min Sik also lived with his parents, my mother and father saw each other quite often, but they didn't speak to each other except for polite greetings.

There was no concept of "dating" in North Korea at that time. Our culture has always been extremely conservative about relations between men and women. If you grow up in the West, you may think that romance occurs naturally, but it does not. You learn how to be romantic from books and movies, or from observation. But there was no model to learn from in my parents' time. They didn't even have the language to talk about their feelings. You just had to guess how your beloved felt from the look in his eyes, or the tone of her voice when she spoke to you. The most they could do was hold hands secretly.

I don't know what my father thought when he met my mother, but she must have been a beautiful sight. She was slender, with strong limbs, high cheekbones, and fine, pale features. She also had a quick mind and a powerful will, which must have fascinated him.

She was not that impressed with him. To her he was ordinary looking, and not very tall. But her brother Min Sik had told her that his friend was capable enough to take care of a wife. There's a saying for men like my father: "He could survive even on bare rock," meaning he was resourceful and resilient no matter what the circumstance.

According to tradition, their marriage was arranged by their families.

My grandfather Park accompanied my father on a selling trip to Kowon. They had decided that it was safer to spread the risk between the two of them, so that neither would be carrying too many cigarettes or too much money if they were searched. When they arrived safely, they stayed with Min Sik and his family.

Grandfather Park quickly noticed my mother, and saw her exchanging significant looks with his son. He sat down with my mother's mother to discuss a match. My parents were judged by their families to be well suited; they both had bad *songbun*. As we say, you have to match swallow with swallow, magpie with magpie. In this case, bride and groom were both magpies. When the deal was done, Jin Sik and Keum Sook were told they were engaged. End of story.

The wedding celebration was nothing special. My mother wore her traditional *hanbok*, and my father came to her parents' house, where there was a big table of food laid out for close family and friends. Then, my mother rode the train to Hyesan for a similar gathering at my father's house. There was no ceremony. My parents just brought their ID cards to the police station to record their marriage, and that was it.

There is another Korean saying: "The thread follows the needle." Usually the man is the needle and the thread is the woman, so the woman follows the husband to his home. But she does not take his name. For many women, it is the only independence that remains in their lives.

Four

Tears of Blood

My parents prospered in the early years of their marriage. They moved into a small house by the railroad station that the military had given to my grandfather after he retired. It was very run-down, but my father started fixing it up for his growing family. My mother became pregnant with my sister, Eunmi, almost right away, and she was born in January 1991.

My father left the metal foundry to find other jobs that gave him more freedom to be away from the office for days at a time to run his businesses. In addition to the cigarettes, he bought sugar, rice, and other goods in the informal markets in Hyesan, then traveled around the country selling them for a profit. When he did business in Wonsan, a port on the East Sea, he brought back dried sand eels—tiny, skinny fish that Koreans love to eat as a side dish. He could sell them for a good profit in our landlocked province, and they became his best-selling product.

Because my mother had spent her whole life in the center of the

country, far away from any outside influences, she didn't know anything about the black market. She didn't even understand the concept
of business. This all changed during the 1990s, when the famine and
an economic collapse turned the whole country into a nation of trad-
ers in order to survive. But before that, capitalism was something
dirty to North Koreans, and money was too disgusting for most people to mention in polite conversation.

Now she was married to a businessman who made his living han-
dling money. It took some getting used to. But like many loyal North
Koreans, she was able to separate her ideology from her actions and
not see that there was much of a conflict. She became a skilled trader
herself. It may have felt unnatural to her at first, but she came to recognize that my father was more aware and competent than other people and she followed his lead. Soon after they were married, she began
helping him buy and sell his products in both the legal and underground markets in Hyesan.

Even though my parents were better off than most of their neighbors, they were never members of the so-called elite. That kind of
wealth came only from high-level government connections. However, they did well enough to take a vacation trip to North Korea's
monument-filled capital, Pyongyang, when Eunmi was an infant, and
my mother was able to dress in some of the fashionable clothes that
were smuggled in from China. She loved designer handbags (even if
they were Chinese knockoffs), Japanese blouses, and nice cosmetics.
Years later, after our escape, I would joke that she was like the Paris
Hilton of North Korea. But she was never extravagant; she just had a
great sense of style.

Despite her good fortune, my mother never stopped working, and
nothing was too difficult for her. She was chopping firewood for the
house late into her pregnancy with Eunmi. The doctors said that's why
she went into labor early and had her first baby in her eighth month.

We think I was even more premature because, in her seventh month, my mother was hauling coal across a railroad bridge in Hyesan.

The coal transport was part of a backdoor enterprise run by my grandfather Park. After he lost his job at the commissary, my grandfather found work as a security guard at a military facility in Hyesan. The building had a stockpile of coal in one storage area, and he would let my parents in to steal it. They had to sneak in at night and carry the coal on their backs through the darkened city. It was hard work and they had to move fast, because if they were caught by the wrong policeman—meaning one they couldn't bribe—they might end up getting arrested. One night on that bridge my mother felt sharp pains in her abdomen, and the next day she delivered a baby the size of a young chicken: me.

According to North Korea, my grandfather Park and my parents were criminals. My father bought and sold goods for a profit; in other countries he'd simply be called a businessman. He bribed officials—whose salaries weren't enough to feed their families—in order to travel freely in his own country. And while it's true that my grandfather and my parents stole from the government, the government stole everything from its people, including their freedom.

As it turns out, my family's business was simply ahead of its time. By the time I was born, in 1993, corruption, bribery, theft, and even market capitalism were becoming a way of life in North Korea as the centralized economy fell apart. The only thing left unchanged when the crisis was over was the regime's brutal, totalitarian grip on political power.

Throughout my childhood, my parents knew that with each passing month it was getting harder and harder to survive in North Korea, but they didn't know why. Foreign media were completely banned in the country, and the newspapers reported only good news about the regime—or blamed all of our hardships on evil plots by our enemies. The truth was that outside our sealed borders, the Communist superpowers that created North Korea were cutting off its lifeline. The big decline started in 1990 when the Soviet Union was breaking apart and Moscow dropped its "friendly rates" for exports to North Korea. Without subsidized fuel and other commodities, the economy creaked to a halt. There was no way for the government to keep the domestic fertilizer factories running, and no fuel for trucks to deliver imported fertilizer to farms. Crop yields dropped sharply. At the same time, Russia almost completely cut off food aid. China helped out for a few years, but it was also going through big changes and increasing its economic ties with capitalist countries—like South Korea and the United States—so it, too, cut off some of its subsidies and started demanding hard currency for exports. North Korea had already defaulted on its bank loans, so it couldn't borrow a penny.

By the time Kim Il Sung died in 1994, famine was already taking hold in the northern provinces. Government rations had been cut sharply, and sometimes they failed to arrive at all.

Instead of changing its policies and reforming its programs, North Korea responded by ignoring the crisis. Instead of opening the country to full international assistance and investment, the regime told the people to eat only two meals a day to preserve our food resources. In his New Year's message of 1995, the new Dear Leader, Kim Jong Il, called on the Korean people to work harder. Although 1994 had brought us "tears of blood," he wrote, we should greet 1995 "energetically, single-mindedly, and with one purpose"—to make the motherland more prosperous.

Unfortunately, our problems could not be fixed with tears and sweat, and the economy went into total collapse after torrential rains caused terrible flooding that wiped out most of the rice harvest. Kim

Jong Il described our national struggle against famine as "The Arduous March," resurrecting the phrase used to describe the hardships his father's generation had faced fighting against the Japanese imperialists. Meanwhile as many as a million North Koreans died from starvation or disease during the worst years of the famine.

The economic collapse disrupted every level of North Korean society. While it had once provided for all our needs, now the regime said it was up to us to save ourselves. When foreign food aid finally started pouring into the country to help famine victims, the government diverted most of it to the military, whose needs always came first. What food did get through to local authorities for distribution quickly ended up being sold on the black market. Suddenly almost everybody in North Korea had to learn to trade or risk starving to death. And the regime realized it had no choice but to tolerate these unofficial markets. In fact, Kim Jong Il eventually allowed permanent, state-managed marketplaces to be built.

The new reality spelled disaster for my father. Now that everyone was buying and selling in the markets, called *jangmadangs*, there was too much competition for him to make a living. Meanwhile, penalties for black market activities grew harsher. As hard as my parents tried to adapt, they were having trouble selling their goods and were falling deeper into debt. My father tried different kinds of businesses. My mother and her friends had an ancient pedal sewing machine they used to patch together pieces of old clothes to make children's clothing. My mother dressed my sister and me in these outfits; her friends sold the rest in the market.

Some people had relatives in China, and they could apply for permits to visit them. My uncle Park Jin did this at least once, but my father didn't because the authorities frowned on it and would have paid closer attention to his business. Those who went almost always came back across the border with things to sell in makeshift stalls on the edges of the *jangmadang*. They told us about the amazing items you could find in the trash in China, even perfectly good clothes. Nothing went to waste in North Korea, and we couldn't imagine throwing anything out that could be used again, even empty plastic bottles, bags, and tin cans. Those were like gold to us.

When you are a very small child, all you know is what is in front of your eyes. Your whole life is your parents, your relatives, your neighborhood. It seemed normal to me that there were times when we had food to eat, and other times when there was only one meal a day and we went hungry.

While they worked to keep us from catastrophe, my parents often had to leave my sister and me alone. If she couldn't find someone to look after us, my mother would have to bolt a metal bar across the door to keep us safe in the house. Sometimes she was away for so long that the sun went down and the house would get dark. My sister, who was afraid of the dark, would cry. I'd say, "Sister, don't cry. *Umma* will be here soon." But after a while, I would lose my nerve and we'd cry together. When we heard her voice at the door, we would run to it, sobbing with relief. It was so hard for my mother to come home and find us like that. But if she had some food, all would be forgotten.

In the free world, children dream about what they want to be when they grow up and how they can use their talents. When I was four and five years old, my only adult ambition was to buy as much bread as I liked and eat all of it. When you are always hungry, all you think about is food. I couldn't understand why my mother would come home with some money and have to save most of it for later. Instead of bread, we would eat only a little bit of porridge or potatoes. My sister and I agreed that if we ever became adults, we would use our money to eat bread until we were full. We would even argue about how much we could eat. She told me she could eat one bucket of bread; I said I could eat ten. She would say ten, I would say one hundred! I thought I could eat a mountain of bread and I would never be filled up.

The worst times were the winters. There was no running water and the river was frozen. There was one pump in town where you could collect fresh water, but you had to line up for hours to fill your bucket. One day when I was about five years old, my mother had to go off to do some business, so she took me there at six in the morning, when it was still dark, to wait in line for her. I stood outside all day in the freezing cold, and by the time she came back for me, it was dark again. I can remember how cold my hands were, and I can still see the bucket and the long line of people in front of me. She has apologized to me for doing that, but I don't blame her for anything; it was what she had to do. For my mother it's still a painful story that lives deep, deep inside her. She carries guilt to this day that she was not better able to enjoy my childhood; she was too busy worrying about getting us enough food to eat.

Despite North Korea's anticapitalist ideals, there were lots of private lenders who got rich by loaning money for monthly interest. My parents borrowed from some of them to keep their business going, but after black market prices collapsed and a lot of their merchandise was confiscated or stolen, they couldn't pay it back. Every night, the people who wanted to collect their debts came to the house while we were eating our meal. They yelled and made threats. Finally, my father decided he couldn't take it anymore. He knew of another way to make money, but it was very dangerous. He had a connection in Pyongyang who could get him some valuable metals—like gold, silver, copper, nickel, and cobalt—that he could sell to the Chinese for a profit.

My mother was against it. When he was selling sand eels and cigarettes, the worst that could happen was that he might have to spend all his profits on bribes, or do a short time in a reeducation camp.

"You can live with that," she told him. "But smuggling stolen metals could get you killed." She was even more frightened when she learned how he intended to bring the contraband to Hyesan. Every passenger train in North Korea had a special cargo car attached at the end of it called Freight Train #9. These #9 trains were exclusively for the use of Kim Jong Il to bring him specialty foods, fruits, and precious materials from different parts of North Korea, and to distribute gifts and necessity items to cadres and party officials around the country. Everything shipped in the special car was sealed in wooden crates that even the police couldn't open to inspect. Nobody could even enter the car without being searched. My father knew somebody who worked on the train, and that man agreed to help smuggle the metals from Pyongyang to Hyesan in one of these safe compartments.

My mother held out for a long time, and then she finally agreed to the plan. It was the only way to survive.

Five

The Dear Leader

Between 1998 and 2002, my father spent most of his time in Pyongyang running the smuggling business. Usually he would be gone for nine months of the year, coming back only for infrequent, short visits when he rode the train to Hyesan along with his latest shipment of metal. My mother quickly learned to run the business in Hyesan, picking up packages from the train and delivering them to the smugglers who sold them across the border in China.

When my father suffered a setback in his business, we would be poor and hungry again, but most of the time things were getting better for us. When he was in town, my father entertained at our house to keep the local officials happy, including the party bosses he paid to ignore his absences from his "official" workplace. My mother cooked big meals of rice and kimchi, grilled meat called *bulgogi*, and other special dishes, while my father filled everyone's glasses to the brim with rice vodka and imported liquor. My father was a captivating story-

teller with a great sense of humor. I fell asleep listening to the sound
of his voice and roars of laughter from the men at the table.

I was just happy when there was food to eat, and we could afford
new shoes and uniforms for school.

I was the smallest kid in my first-grade class, and definitely not the
smartest. I know this because in North Korea they line you up by
your height, and seat you in class by your test scores. I had trouble
learning how to read and write and needed special help. I hated being
at the bottom of the class, and sometimes just refused to go to school.

I had a headstrong personality, perhaps because I had to work so
hard for everything I achieved. I was determined to learn how to
read, so I struggled to make sense of all those characters swimming
across the page.

When my father was home, he would sometimes hold me in his
lap and read me children's books. I loved stories, but the only books
available in North Korea were published by the government and had
political themes. Instead of scary fairy tales, we had stories set in a
filthy and disgusting place called South Korea, where homeless children went barefoot and begged in the streets. It never occurred to me
until after I arrived in Seoul that those books were really describing
life in North Korea. But we couldn't see past the propaganda.

When I finally learned to read by myself, I couldn't get enough
books to satisfy me. Again, most of them were about our Leaders and
how they worked so hard and sacrificed so much for the people. One
of my favorites was a biography of Kim Il Sung. It described how he
suffered as a young man while fighting the Japanese imperialists, surviving by eating frogs and sleeping in the snow.

In the classroom every subject we learned—math, science, reading, music—was delivered with a dose of propaganda. Kim Il Sung's son, our Dear Leader Kim Jong Il, showed incredible loyalty to his father, and this was an example for schoolchildren. In class we read a textbook about how Kim Il Sung was so busy leading our nation that he would have to read documents while riding in his car. But this was hard because the road was bumpy and the pages would shake. But when Kim Jong Il was very young, he managed to cover the road with loads of sand to make the ride smooth and comfortable for his father.

Our Dear Leader had mystical powers. His biography said he could control the weather with his thoughts, and that he wrote fifteen hundred books during his three years at Kim Il Sung University. Even when he was a child he was an amazing tactician, and when he played military games, his team always won because he came up with brilliant new strategies every time. That story inspired my classmates in Hyesan to play military games, too. But nobody ever wanted to be on the American imperialist team, because they would always have to lose the battle.

In school, we sang a song about Kim Jong Il and how he worked so hard to give our laborers on-the-spot instruction as he traveled around the country, sleeping in his car and eating only small meals of rice balls. "Please, please, Dear Leader, take a good rest for us!" we sang through our tears. "We are all crying for you."

This worship of the Kims was reinforced in documentaries, movies, and shows broadcast by the single, state-run television station. Whenever the Leaders' smiling pictures appeared on the screen, stirring sentimental music would build in the background. It made me so emotional every time. North Koreans are raised to venerate our fathers and our elders; it's part of the culture we inherited from Confucianism. And so in our collective minds, Kim Il Sung was our beloved grandfather and Kim Jong Il was our father.

Once I even dreamed about Kim Jong Il. He was smiling and hugging me and giving me candy. I woke up so happy, and for a long time the memory of that dream was the biggest joy in my life.

Jang Jin Sung, a famous North Korea defector and former poet laureate who worked in North Korea's propaganda bureau, calls this phenomenon "emotional dictatorship." In North Korea, it's not enough for the government to control where you go, what you learn, where you work, and what you say. They need to control you through your emotions, making you a slave to the state by destroying your individuality, and your ability to react to situations based on your own experience of the world.

This dictatorship, both emotional and physical, is reinforced in every aspect of your life. In fact, the indoctrination starts as soon as you learn to talk and are taken on your mother's back to the *inminban* meetings everybody in North Korea has to attend at least once a week. You learn that your friends are your "comrades" and that is how you address one another. You are taught to think with one mind.

As soon as you are in school you are drilled in the 10 Principles of the regime, like the Ten Commandments of the Bible. (Number 1: "We must give our all in the struggle to unify the entire society with the revolutionary ideology of the Great Leader comrade Kim Il Sung." Number 2: "Respect the Great Leader respected comrade Kim Il Sung with the utmost loyalty." . . . Number 10: "We must pass down the great achievements of Great Leader comrade Kim Il Sung's revolution from generation to generation, inheriting and completing it to the end.") You learn the principle of *juche*, or national self-determination. And you are taught to hate the enemies of the state with a burning passion.

Our classrooms and schoolbooks were plastered with images of grotesque American GIs with blue eyes and huge noses executing civilians or being vanquished with spears and bayonets by brave young

Korean children. Sometimes during recess from school we lined up to take turns beating or stabbing dummies dressed up like American soldiers. I was so scared that the Yankee devils would attack us again and torture me to death in the most evil way.

In second grade we were taught simple math, but not the way it is taught in other countries. In North Korea, even arithmetic is a propaganda tool. A typical problem would go like this: "If you kill one American bastard and your comrade kills two, how many dead American bastards do you have?"

We could never just say "American"—that would be too respectful. It had to be "American bastard," "Yankee devil," or "big-nosed Yankee." If you didn't say it, you would be criticized for being too soft on our enemies.

Likewise, any mention of the Kims had to be preceded by a title or tender description to show our infinite love and respect for our Leaders. One time when my mother was preparing food in the kitchen and I grabbed a newspaper, I had to read it for a long time before I realized I had just finished the title of our Leader: "Our great comrade Kim Jong Il, the general secretary of the Workers' Party of Korea, the chairman of the DPRK National Defense Commission, and the supreme commander of the Korean People's Army, said today . . ."

I don't think my father was brainwashed the way the rest of us were. My mother has told me he was more aware of what the regime was doing to its people. I heard him grumble about it only once, and I didn't understand what my father was saying at the time. We were listening to the television news broadcast with the usual footage of Kim Jong Il inspecting troops somewhere. The newsreaders were going on and on about how much the Dear Leader was suffering in the cold to give his benevolent guidance to the loyal soldiers when my father snapped, "That son of a bitch! Turn off the TV."

My mother whispered furiously, "Be careful what you say around

the children! This isn't just about what you think. You're putting all
of us in danger."

I had no idea my father was talking about Kim Jong Il. I could
never imagine showing disrespect for the regime or our Leaders. That
would be unthinkable.

My father wasn't the only one who was beginning to think differently.

In fact, capitalism was already alive and well just a few blocks
away in the bustling *jangmadang*. Only a few years earlier, the market
had consisted of a few grandmothers selling homegrown vegetables
and snacks. Now a corrugated metal roof covered rows and rows of
market stalls where vendors sold everything from handmade rice
cakes to Chinese athletic shoes. If you knew where to look, you could
also find things like digital watches and DVD players from vendors
who operated in the gray area between legal and illegal trade in the
new North Korea.

The smugglers who brought the black market goods back and forth
to China lived in low houses behind the market, along the river's
edge. I got to know this neighborhood well. When my father was in
town with a shipment from Pyongyang, he would sometimes hide
the metal in my little book bag, and then carry me piggyback from
our house to one of the smugglers' shacks. From there some men took
the package to Chinese buyers on the other side of the river. Sometimes the smugglers would wade or walk across the Yalu River, sometimes they met their Chinese counterparts halfway. They did it at
night, signaling one another with flashlights. There were so many of
them doing business that each needed a special code—one, two,
three flashes—so they didn't get one another mixed up.

The soldiers who guarded the border were part of the operation by now, and they were always there to take their cut. Of course, even with the authorities looking the other way, there still were many things that you were forbidden to buy or sell. And breaking the rules could be fatal.

In North Korea, public executions were used to teach us lessons in loyalty to the regime and the consequences of disobedience. In Hyesan when I was little, a young man was executed right behind the market for killing and eating a cow. It was a crime to eat beef without special permission. Cows were the property of the state, and were too valuable to eat because they were used for plowing fields and dragging carts, so anybody who butchered one would be stealing government property.

The young man had committed some other petty crimes, but the cow was his main offense. He suffered from tuberculosis and had nothing to eat, but that didn't make any difference to the police. They announced his execution to the whole city, and then brought him to the market and tied him at the chest, knees, and ankles to a heavy piece of wood. Three men with rifles stood in front of him and began firing. The executioners tried to cut the ropes with bullets and it took a long time. Finally, they succeeded, and the dead man flopped to the ground. My mother watched in shock as they rolled the body away, stuffed it into a sack, and drove it off in the back of a truck. Her blood went cold and she was unable to move her legs for a while. She couldn't believe that in her own country a human's life had less value than an animal's. Even a dog would be treated with more respect.

There was an endless list of crimes in North Korea. The government was obsessed with preventing corrupt ideas from penetrating our borders, so all foreign media were totally forbidden. Although many families owned televisions, radios, and VCR players, they were allowed to listen to or watch only state-generated news programs and propaganda films, which were incredibly boring. There was a huge demand for foreign movies and South Korean television shows, even though you never knew when the police might raid your house searching for smuggled media. First they would shut off the electricity (if the power was on in the first place) so that the videocassette or DVD would be trapped in the machine when they came through the door. But people learned to get around this by owning two video players and quickly switching them out if they heard a police team coming. If you were caught smuggling or distributing illegal videos, the punishment could be severe. Some people have even been executed by firing squad—just to set an example for the rest of us.

Radios and televisions came sealed and permanently tuned to state-approved channels. If you tampered with them, you could be arrested and sent to a labor camp for reeducation, but a lot of people did it anyway. In the border areas those of us with receivers could sometimes pick up Chinese television broadcasts. I was mostly interested in the food commercials. There were advertisements for exotic things like milk and cookies. I never drank milk in North Korea! I didn't even know it came from a cow until after I escaped. My friends and I would watch these incredible things and understand that the Chinese had more, but it never really occurred to us that our lives could be any different.

I'm often asked why people would risk going to prison to watch Chinese commercials or South Korean soap operas or year-old wrestling matches. I think it's because people are so oppressed in North Korea, and daily life is so grim and colorless, that people are desperate for any kind of escape. When you watch a movie, your imagination can carry you away for two whole hours. You come back refreshed, your struggles temporarily forgotten.

My uncle Park Jin had a VCR, and when I was very young, I would go to his house to watch tapes of Hollywood movies. My aunt covered the windows and told us not to say anything about it. I loved *Cinderella*,

Snow White, and James Bond movies. But when I was seven or eight years old, the film that changed my life was *Titanic*. It amazed me that it was a story that took place a hundred years ago. Those people living in 1912 had better technology than most North Koreans! But mostly I couldn't believe how someone could make a movie out of such a shameful love story. In North Korea, the filmmakers would have been executed. No real human stories were allowed, nothing but propaganda about the Leader. But in *Titanic*, the characters talked about love and humanity. I was amazed that Leonardo DiCaprio and Kate Winslet were willing to die for love, not just for the regime, as we were. The idea that people could choose their own destinies fascinated me. This pirated Hollywood movie gave me my first small taste of freedom.

But while the outside media offered me a glimpse of a larger world very different from the one I occupied, I never imagined I could live like the characters in those movies. I couldn't look at the people on the screen and think they were real, or allow myself to envy their lives. The propaganda we were fed inoculated me from any lessons I might apply to my own life. It also made me numb to the suffering that was going on all around me as the famine was taking its terrible toll.

North Koreans have two stories running in their heads at all times, like trains on parallel tracks. One is what you are taught to believe; the other is what you see with your own eyes. It wasn't until I escaped to South Korea and read a translation of George Orwell's *Nineteen Eighty-Four* that I found a word for this peculiar condition: *doublethink*. This is the ability to hold two contradictory ideas in your mind at the same time—and somehow not go crazy.

This "doublethink" is how you can shout slogans denouncing capitalism in the morning, then browse through the market in the afternoon to buy smuggled South Korean cosmetics.

It is how you can believe that North Korea is a socialist paradise, the best country in the world with the happiest people who have nothing to envy, while devouring movies and TV programs that show ordinary people in enemy nations enjoying a level of prosperity that you couldn't imagine in your dreams.

It is how you can sit in Hyesan watching propaganda videos showing productive factories, supermarkets stocked with food, and well-dressed people in amusement parks and believe you are living on the same planet as your government Leaders.

It is how you can recite the motto "Children Are King" in school, then walk home past the orphanage where children with bloated bellies stare at you with hungry eyes.

Maybe deep, deep inside me I knew something was wrong. But we North Koreans can be experts at lying, even to ourselves. The frozen babies that starving mothers abandoned in the alleys did not fit into my worldview, so I couldn't process what I saw. It was normal to see bodies in the trash heaps, bodies floating in the river, normal to just walk by and do nothing when a stranger cried for help.

There are images I can never forget. Late one afternoon, my sister and I found the body of a young man lying beside a pond. It was a place where people went to fetch water, and he must have dragged himself there to drink. He was naked and his eyes were staring and his mouth wide open in an expression of terrible suffering. I had seen many dead bodies before, but this was the most horrible and frightening of all, because his insides were coming out where something—maybe dogs—had ripped him open. I was so embarrassed for him, lying there stripped of his clothes and his dignity. I could not bear to look at him, so I grabbed my sister's hand and we ran home.

My mother tried to help people when she could. Homeless wanderers would sometimes knock on our door to beg for food. I remember one young woman who brought her daughter to our house. "I'm so cold, so hungry," she said. "But if you give me food, I'll let my baby eat." My mother understood that feeling because she had young children, too. She invited them inside and gave them both plates of food. I watched them closely, because the daughter was nearly my age. They were very polite, and ate delicately even though they were starving. I wonder often if they survived, and if they are still in North Korea.

There were so many desperate people on the streets crying for help that you had to shut off your heart or the pain would be too much. After a while you can't care anymore. And that is what hell is like.

Almost everybody I knew lost family in the famine. The youngest and oldest died first. Then the men, who had fewer reserves than women. Starving people wither away until they can no longer fight off diseases, or the chemicals in their blood become so unbalanced that their hearts forget to beat.

My own family suffered, too, as our fortune rose and fell like a cork in the ocean. In 1999, my father tried to use trucks instead of trains to smuggle metals out of Pyongyang, but there were too many expenses to pay drivers and buy gasoline, too many checkpoints and too many bribes to pay, so he ended up losing all of his money. My mother took me and my sister with her to live with her relatives for a few months while my father went back to his train business and made up his losses.

We arrived in Kowon to find that my mother's family was also struggling to survive. Grandfather Byeon had died a few years earlier, and my grandmother was living with her older son, Min Sik, in the family home. Her youngest son, Jong Sik, who had been imprisoned years earlier for stealing from the state, was visiting them as well. In the labor camp he had caught tuberculosis, which was very common in North Korea. Now that there was so little food to go around, he was sick all the time and wasting away.

My grandmother had taken in lots of neighborhood children, and in order to make sure everybody else was fed, she ate only a tiny bit of food each day. She worried that she was a burden, even though she consumed so little and her bones were as light as a bird's.

I loved my little grandmother Hwang with her wooden leg. She never got upset with me, even when I cried and pestered her to carry me on her back like a horse. She always smiled at me and she was a wonderful storyteller; I would sit with her for hours as she told me about her childhood in the South. She described a beautiful island off the southern coast called Jeju, where women divers can hold their breath for a long time and swim like fish while they gather food from the bottom of the sea. I was so curious when she described the wide blue ocean to me, and the playful dolphins that lived there. I had never seen an ocean or heard of such a thing as a dolphin. Once I asked her, "Grandma, what is the biggest thing in the world?" She told me it was the whale that breathes in air from a hole in its back and makes a fountain come out. I had never even seen pictures of whales, but they sounded like something I would like.

Most of her stories were from the time of Chosun, when there was no North or South Korea, only one country, one people. She told me we had the same culture and shared the same traditions as the South. She also told me a little bit about the time she visited Seoul, although even saying the name was forbidden in North Korea. You just didn't mention such an evil place. I knew it existed only from propaganda, newspaper articles describing anti-imperialist demonstrations by its oppressed masses. But somehow my grandmother planted deep inside me a curiosity about this place she had loved. She told me, "Come to my grave someday, and tell me that the North and South are reunited."

It was a sad time to visit Kowon; because of the famine, so many people were dying. My grandmother took a lot of medicines, some opium for the pains of old age and other pills to help her sleep and forget the suffering around her. One morning before I went out to play, I saw her take lots of her medicine, much more than usual.

"Grandma, why are you taking so much medicine?" I asked.

She was very calm and smiled at me. "Grandma just wants to have a good sleep," she said. "She needs a good rest."

Later that afternoon, I heard a terrible sound coming from the house. It was my uncle Jong Sik calling my grandmother's name. We ran inside and he was shaking her in her bed, wailing, "Wake up! Wake up! Answer me!"

But she was lying there peacefully, and no matter how loud my uncle shouted, she could no longer hear him.

A few months later, my uncle would also be dead. Sometimes I can still hear his voice, screaming for his mother, begging her to wake up. These are some of the things I wish I could forget, but I know I never will.

Six

City of Dreams

B y the year 2000, when I turned seven years old, my father's business was thriving. We had returned to Hyesan after my grandmother's funeral and, before long, my family was rich—at least by our standards. We ate rice three times a day and meat two or three times a month. We had money for medical emergencies, new shoes, and things like shampoo and toothpaste that were beyond the means of ordinary North Koreans. We still didn't have a telephone, car, or motorbike, but our lives seemed very luxurious to our friends and neighbors.

My father came back from his business trips with loads of gifts for us. He brought my sister and me new clothes and books; my mother would get perfume and face powder. But his most exciting black market purchase was a 1980s-era Nintendo set for playing video games.

My favorite was Super Mario Bros. Whenever the electricity was on, I sat for hours moving the little characters across the screen to bouncy, happy music that still makes me smile when I hear it. My parents loved playing video tennis games, and they could be quite competitive. It was fun to watch them act like kids with the controls in their hands, shouting playful insults at each other. They were also obsessed with professional wrestling videos, which they would watch together in the darkened room after my sister and I had gone to bed. We could hear both of them yelling, "Hit him harder!" My mother's favorite was a huge blond woman wrestler who defeated all her rivals. But I didn't like watching these videos because of all the violence. We had enough of that on the streets and at home.

M y parents had a complicated and passionate marriage. They respected each other and were great partners. They made each other laugh. When my father was sober, he treated my mother like gold. But when he was drinking, it was a different story.

North Korean society is by its nature tough and violent, and so are relations between men and women. The woman is expected to obey her father and her husband; males always come first in everything. When I was growing up, women could not sit at the same table with men. Many of my neighbors' and classmates' houses had special bowls and spoons for their fathers. It was commonplace for a husband to beat his wife. We had one neighbor whose husband was so brutal that she couldn't click her chopsticks while she ate for fear he would hit her for making noise.

By comparison, my father was an enlightened man. He included my mother and my sister and me at the table; he respected us. He drank only occasionally and rarely beat my mother. But sometimes he did. I am not excusing his actions, but I am explaining the culture— men in North Korea were taught they were superior, just as they were taught to obey our Leader.

The difference in our household was that my mother wouldn't

take it. Unlike many North Korean women, who would cry and apologize, my mother hit back. She had a strong spirit, stronger than my father's, and he was no match for her. When their fights got out of control, I would run down the street to get the neighbors to break it up. Sometimes I was afraid they would kill each other.

During their worst fights, my mother would sometimes threaten divorce, but they quickly reconciled. It wasn't until another woman entered my father's life that my mother almost left for good.

When my father began his business in Pyongyang, he needed a place to stay and an assistant to help him with his work. His older sister lived in the city and she introduced him to a single woman in her early twenties named Wan Sun. She was available to work as his assistant, plus she lived with her family in a large apartment with an extra room that he could rent. That's where he stayed for nine months of the year.

As it turned out, theirs was more than just a working relationship, although my father always tried to deny it. Still, it was not unusual for a wealthy or powerful man to take a mistress in North Korea. After a while, Wan Sun fell in love and wanted to marry him. But first she had to get rid of my mother. It was like a plot from a bad South Korean soap opera—and it almost worked.

In August 2001, my mother decided to go to Pyongyang for a few months while my father spent some time with us in Hyesan. Naturally, she stayed in Wan Sun's apartment while she sold a few products on the black market and bought some metals to sell in Hyesan. What she didn't know was that Wan Sun was calling my father and telling him that his wife was seeing other men. Unfortunately, he believed these lies, and the next time my mother and father spoke on the telephone he accused her of cheating. She couldn't understand why he was saying such things. She was so upset and angry that she told him she wanted a divorce.

This time she meant it. Instead of returning to Hyesan, she took the next train to Kowon to visit her brother Min Sik and think about her next move.

When my mother didn't come home, my father realized his mistake and was very unhappy. He even started drinking every day, which was unusual for him. Then one afternoon, about two weeks after my mother had run away to Kowon, I answered a knock on the door and found an unfamiliar young woman standing outside, dressed in fancy city clothes. This was my first glimpse of Wan Sun. As soon as she found out that my mother had asked for a divorce, she was on the next train to Hyesan. I had no idea what was going on, but it all seemed very strange.

Later that day, it got even stranger when my friend Yong Ja poked her head in the door and asked me to come over to her house to play. When I stepped inside, my mother was waiting there for me. I was so happy to see her again that I ran into her arms.

"Yeonmi-ya! I missed you so much!" she said.

I still had no clue why she had left and then returned without warning, but she later told me what had happened. Her brother had agreed to take her in if she divorced my father—but only if she left her children behind. She couldn't abandon us, and during her time away from my father, she began to remember all the good things about him. So she had returned to her family to mend things.

"How is your father, Yeonmi?" she asked.

"Right now he is home with a lady from Pyongyang," I said.

"Stay right here and don't come back home until I send for you," she said.

When she reached our house, she found Wan Sun sitting on a floor mat inside, talking to my father. I don't know whether my father or his girlfriend was more surprised to see my mother standing in the doorway. My mother ran in and kicked Wan Sun right in the butt, yelling, "Get out of my house!" Wan Sun stood up and slapped her, and my father had to hold my mother to keep her from tearing Wan Sun to pieces. My father told Wan Sun she had better go, and my mother slammed the door behind her.

It was the beginning of November, and this skinny girl from Pyongyang wasn't prepared for the freezing weather. She was wearing a light coat and thin, impractical shoes. Wan Sun stood outside our house like a shivering ghost, whimpering for my father to let her in again.

Meanwhile, my father begged my mother to change her mind and not divorce him. He still swore to her that nothing was going on between him and his assistant. My mother didn't know what to believe. But she knew that her family was more important than this woman, so she decided to stay. Wan Sun left on the next train back to Pyongyang.

If you asked anyone in the North Korean countryside, "What is your dream?" most would answer, "To see Pyongyang in my lifetime."

I was eight years old when that dream came true for me.

Only the most privileged citizens are allowed to live and work in the nation's capital. You need special permission even to visit. But Pyongyang is as familiar to ordinary North Koreans as our own backyards because of the hundreds upon hundreds of picture books and propaganda films that celebrate it as the perfect expression of our socialist paradise. To us, it is a mystical shrine with towering monuments and thrilling pageantry—like Red Square, Jerusalem, and Disneyland all in one city.

My father had not been home in a long time, so he invited each of his daughters to visit him for one month in the summer. I went first. The idea of seeing my father and the city of my dreams at the same time was so exciting that I couldn't sleep for a whole week before he arrived to pick me up. It was especially exciting because 2002 was the first summer that North Korea staged its now-famous Arirang Festival, a massive celebration of the regime's military and cultural prowess. I could not believe I would actually get to see it all with my own eyes. I told all my neighbors and classmates about my trip. Some parents asked me not to brag in front of their children, because now they were begging to visit Pyongyang, too.

I packed all my best clothes including my Princess T-shirt and my Mary Jane shoes for this special trip. My father and I left on the morning train for Pyongyang. Even though the distance was only about 225 miles, the ride took days, because electricity shortages slowed down the train. My father and I brought food with us and traveled in a sleeper car, but most people had to sleep on hard seats. When the train finally pulled into the Pyongyang station, Wan Sun came to greet us. I still didn't understand what the trouble was all about when she was in Hyesan a few months before, and in fact I hardly remembered her. But I had a child's sense that something was off about this arrangement as I watched her take my father's arm. That feeling passed quickly, however, as I was carried away by the spellbinding sights and sounds of Pyongyang.

Everything amazed me. I took my first ride on a public bus that day, and I was astonished that people were also traveling around in an underground subway, and in private cars. I had never seen a taxi before, and my father had to help me pronounce a word for it and explain what it meant. Even crazier was a new kind of drink my father bought for me. It was a very bright color and came in a bottle, but when I drank it, it was not gentle in my mouth—in fact, it was painful, like an electric shock.

"*Abuji*, I don't like this," I told my father as I blinked back tears.

"Come on, now," he said softly. "Don't act like a country girl! If you drink more, you'll like it." But that fizzy soda scared me so much that I never wanted to try another.

Pyongyang felt like a fairyland to me. Everybody seemed so clean and well dressed. Because of an order by Kim Jong Il, all the women had to wear skirts. In Hyesan, a lot of women ignored the official dress code and wore more practical slacks, but not in this fancy city. To me, the residents seemed more refined, with gentler accents and more polite ways of talking than the tough, guttural language we used in the far north.

In contrast to the crumbling apartment houses, dusty alleys, and sooty rail yards of Hyesan, Pyongyang seemed so new and shiny, with huge buildings and wide, spotless boulevards. You hardly saw anyone begging here, just the street children we called *kotjebi*, who haunted the markets and train stations in every part of North Korea. The difference in Pyongyang was that whenever the *kotjebi* asked for food or money, the police officers came and drove them off.

Wherever we went, my father pleaded with me to hold his hand tightly. He was afraid I would get lost because I was always looking up at the giant city all around me. When he took me on a bus ride at night to see the lights of downtown Pyongyang, I nearly lost my mind. The only thing that was ever lit up at night in Hyesan was the Kim Il Sung monument, but here all the important buildings glowed like torches. There were so many propaganda banners, some of them written in neon, saying "Pyongyang, Heart of Korea." That was impressive enough, but even the restaurant signs were neon.

We visited all the sights I had only read about or seen on television: My father showed me the famous Ryugyong Hotel, a 105-story pyramid in the center of the city, designed to be the tallest hotel in the world but never finished. (It's still not finished.) We posed for a picture in front of the graceful Mansudae fountains on "The Hill of the Sun," where I laid flowers at the feet of the giant bronze statue of

Kim Il Sung. The Great Leader smiled at his people from seventy-five feet above the enormous plaza. He was dressed in a long top coat, with one arm raised as if to reveal the nation's destiny. My father, always the joker, remarked to Wan Sun, "How cool would it be to take off his big coat and sell it in China?" Then he added, "Or at least one of his shoes."

My father said the most surprising things. I realize now that he was like Winston Smith in *Nineteen Eighty-Four*, a man who secretly saw past Big Brother's propaganda and knew how things really worked in the country. But I was still years away from understanding that the Kims weren't gods. I had a warm, holy feeling being in Pyongyang, where the Great Leader once walked, and where his son, Kim Jong Il, now lived. Just knowing he breathed the same air made me feel so proud and special—which is exactly how I was supposed to feel.

One day we took a two-hour boat ride down the Taedong River to visit Kim Il Sung's birthplace at Mangyongdae, but changed our minds and instead went to a good Chinese restaurant nearby. I had never been in a restaurant where you sat in chairs. In Hyesan, we could sometimes eat food at the market, and there were a few places like restaurants in people's houses, but you always sat on the floor. Sitting in a stiff chair seemed very odd to me—and I will still always sit on the floor if I have a choice. But I really liked ordering all kinds of food from a waitress and having someone put it in front of me. For the first time, I ate bread that was soft and delicate instead of black and hard. I finally got to taste those oily noodles I had smelled cooking across the river in China, but I was not used to the flavor. I didn't say anything, but I almost wished I'd had some kimchi instead. But I ate thinly sliced pork and some other delicious Chinese dishes that were like heaven on earth. In the future, whenever I was hungry, I would eat this meal a thousand times over in my mind. My only regret was that I didn't order more food.

. . . .

W an Sun's apartment was on the eleventh floor of a high-rise apartment building in the Songyo district in eastern Pyongyang. I took the first elevator ride of my life in that building. I had seen these things in movies and South Korean soap operas, but the actual experience was more scary than exciting. The electricity in the building worked, but they kept the lights off in the hallways and elevator to save power. So I just held tightly to my father's hand while we felt our way through the lobby and up to the apartment.

Once inside, there were lots of windows and lights to see everything, There were three bedrooms, one bath, a kitchen, and a big dining area. Wan Sun's father and stepmother slept in one bedroom, Wan Sun stayed with her two younger sisters in a second bedroom, and I slept with my father in the third. At least that's how it was while I was visiting. As soon as we arrived at the apartment, my father stretched out on his bed after the long train ride. Wan Sun sat down right next to him and leaned against him. It made me uncomfortable, because that's what I had seen my mother and father do. So I crawled in between them and snuggled up to my father.

Just about every morning we woke up to the sound of the national anthem blaring on the government-supplied radio. Every household in North Korea had to have one, and you could never turn it off. It was tuned to only one station, and that's how the government could control you even when you were in your own home. In the morning it played lots of enthusiastic songs with titles like "Strong and Prosperous Nation," reminding us how lucky we were to celebrate our proud socialist life. I was surprised that the radio was on so much in Pyongyang. Back home, the electricity was usually off, so we had to wake ourselves up.

At seven in the morning, there was always a lady knocking on the door of the apartment in Pyongyang, yelling, "Get up! Time to clean!" She was head of the *inminban*, or "people's unit," that included every apartment in our part of the building. In North Korea, everybody is required to wake up early and spend an hour sweeping and scrubbing the hallways, or tending the area outside their houses. Communal labor is how we keep up our revolutionary spirit and work together as one people. The regime wants us to be like cells in a single organism, where no unit can exist without the others. We have to do everything at the same time, always. So at noon, when the radio goes "*beeeep*," everybody stops to eat lunch. There is no getting away from it.

After the people of Pyongyang finish cleaning in the morning, they line up for the buses and go off to work. In the northern provinces, not many people were going to work anymore because there was nothing left to do. The factories and mines had stopped operating and there was nothing to manufacture. Even if the men went to their offices or assembly lines they would just drink, play cards, and gamble. But Pyongyang was different. Everybody seemed busy. One time Wan Sun's little sister took me to visit the factory where she worked, a place where they made plastic for car tires. It was the only factory I saw in North Korea that actually functioned.

I had other exciting adventures during my month in Pyongyang. We got tickets to several of the huge Arirang Festival performances in the giant May Day Stadium. I was overwhelmed by the spectacular dramatic, musical, and gymnastic presentations. Most impressive were the thirty thousand to fifty thousand schoolchildren who had trained for many months to sit in the risers behind the stage, holding up colored squares like a living mural to create enormous, ever-changing scenes and slogans glorifying the regime. Only much later did I realize how abusive it was for these children to perform for hours and hours without even a small break to eat or use the bathroom. We were taught that it was an honor to suffer for our leaders, who had suffered so much for us. Given the chance, I would proudly have joined them.

I also visited a zoo for the first time in my life and saw monkeys, tigers, bears, and elephants. It was like stepping into one of my picture books. The most exciting animal I saw was a peacock. I didn't think these birds were real, just drawings somebody made up. But when the male peacock spread his magnificent tail feathers, I nearly screamed. I couldn't imagine it was possible for something so beautiful to exist in the same world as me.

As the weeks went by, Wan Sun went out of her way to be nice to me, so I actually liked her after a while. And my father was very good to her. When they first met, she was suffering from tuberculosis, which was common even among the elite. He made sure she ate well and got the right medicines. She was almost cured by the time I met her. Looking back at it, I think he must have had feelings for her, but like so many other things in my life, I preferred not to see what was in front of me.

One time I woke up in the middle of the night and heard people arguing. Instead of sleeping in the bed next to me, my father was in the other room with Wan Sun, who was crying and pleading with him.

"Why don't you get divorced!" I heard her say. "I can take care of Yeonmi, she's small. Let Eunmi stay with her mother."

My father whispered furiously, "Don't say that! You're going to wake her up!"

Later, my father made me promise not to tell my mother about any of this when I returned to Hyesan.

Toward the end of my stay, my father became very sick with stomach pains and he decided to check into the Red Cross hospital in Pyongyang for tests. They couldn't find what was wrong at that hospital, so he went to the most modern hospital in the capital, where the elites go for treatment. Even the best doctors in the country couldn't tell him why he was sick, so he gave up trying to figure it out and decided to bring me home.

We rode on the train to Hyesan, along with his latest shipment of metal. As we rolled through the stations, the mountains got steeper and the landscape grew harder and poorer. The bright lights and clean streets of Pyongyang faded back into a dream as I looked out the window and saw skinny peasants scraping the dirt with their hoes, picking up whatever seeds and grain they could find.

Whenever the train stopped, the *kotjebi* street children would climb up and knock on my window to beg. I could see them scrambling to pick up any spoiled food that people threw away, even moldy grains of rice. My father was worried that they would get sick eating bad food and told me we shouldn't give them our garbage. I saw that some of those children were about my age, and many even younger. But I can't say I felt compassion or even pity, just simple curiosity about how they managed to survive eating all that rotten food. As we pulled away from the station, some of them were still hanging on, holding tight to the undercarriage, using all their energy not to fall off the running train and looking up at me with eyes that had no curiosity or even anger. What I saw in them was a pure determination to live, an animal instinct for survival even when there seemed to be no hope.

Before we reached Hyesan, the train stopped suddenly between stations. People were saying that one of the street kids had crawled onto the roof of the train and was killed when he touched a live wire. We were delayed while they removed the body, and some people seemed annoyed. Otherwise the incident didn't seem to bother anyone.

My mother picked us up at the station while my father went to pay the policeman guarding the #9 Freight car and then pick up his package. I was so happy to be home, and to see our familiar house and my garden of sunflowers. I had missed my mother so much and I couldn't wait to tell her everything that happened in Pyongyang.

"Did you see the Juche Tower, Yeonmi-ya?" my mother said as she made me a rice cake. "And all the monuments?"

"Yes, *Umma*! We went everywhere with Wan Sun."

"Really?" my mother said with a very cool voice.

"Yes," I said. "And we went to the zoo, too!"

But I didn't say any more.

E unmi went back to Pyongyang with my father, and then returned home with him at the end of the summer. While he was in Hyesan, my father got a call through to Wan Sun and heard some troubling news. It turned out she was doing some side business helping another smuggler in Pyongyang, and that smuggler had informed on her. The police had picked her up for questioning, but she ran away during a break in her interrogation. Now she was in hiding.

Before my father left to return to Pyongyang, my mother warned him to stay away from Wan Sun from now on. She told him that girl was trouble.

But he did not listen.

Seven

The Darkest Nights

My father returned to Pyongyang at the end of October 2002, and before long he had another shipment of metal ready to go to China. All that was missing was a burlap sack and some rope to prepare the package for the train to Hyesan. Those items were hard to find, even in the capital, but my father knew somebody in town who usually had a good supply.

Ignoring my mother's advice, and his own good sense, he had contacted Wan Sun after he arrived in Pyongyang. Apparently she was still helping him with his business because Wan Sun went to purchase the rope and sack while he waited at a nearby market. What they didn't know was that detectives from the prosecutor's office—which has its own investigators—were watching the house, probably because they had received a tip that Wan Sun and possibly my father would be arriving.

My father waited for about an hour, and when Wan Sun didn't

return, he went looking for her. The detectives had set a trap for him at the house, but they didn't arrest him right away. Instead they followed him, hoping he would lead them to his cache of illegal metals. But when they saw he was about to get on a bus and disappear, they grabbed him.

"Are you Park Jin Sik?" one of them demanded.

"Yes," my father said. And with that each took one of his arms and placed him under arrest.

Later, when my mother tried to piece together what happened, she learned that the police had arrested a copper smuggler in Pyongyang who knew about my father's operation. During her interrogation, she told the police that she could name two other people buying stolen metals, a "big fish" from Hyesan named Park Jin Sik who worked with a young girl from Pyongyang.

Wan Sun was arrested at the same time as my father and sentenced to six months in a labor "training" camp. We heard that she got married to a former military officer after she finished her sentence, and had a baby with him. I was happy to hear that she was able to put her troubles behind her. Like everybody else, she was just trying to survive.

Sadly, my father would pay a much bigger price for his crimes against the state.

In November 2002, my mother came back from a visit to the post office crying and shaking. I didn't understand why until I heard her talking to my friend Yong Ja's grandmother. My mother told her she had tried to call my father in Pyongyang but couldn't reach him. That's when she found out he had been arrested for smuggling.

My mother hoped it was all a mistake, or even a bad dream. But she knew she had to act quickly. She needed to travel to the capital to find out where my father was being held, and to see if she could pay enough money to get him out of jail.

The morning my mother left for Pyongyang, she sat down with me and my sister to explain what had happened, and what was going to happen next. She warned us that people would treat us differently now.

"They might say bad things about our family," she said. "But please try not to let it bother you too much. Your father will come home soon and will protect us." She told us we had nothing to be ashamed of, so we should laugh out loud like always, and act as if nothing was wrong.

She kneeled before Eunmi and said, "You are the first child, and so you are the pillar of this house while I am away." Then she turned to me and said, "Yeonmi, you have to help Eunmi."

She left us with a bag of rice and some cooking oil. She told us there would be no money coming for a while, and that we couldn't eat like before. We had to save everything now, and not waste even one grain.

We walked her to the station, and as she was about to board the train, she gave us about 200 won, enough for a bit of dried beans or corn if we ran out of rice. "I'll be back as soon as I can, and I'll bring more food," she said. Then she hugged us good-bye. We watched for a long time as the train pulled away. I was only eight years old, but I felt like my childhood was departing with her.

On the way back to our house Eunmi and I saw someone selling food on the street. We stared for a long time at the candy and imported snacks from China. Our mother had never let us have these treats because they were so expensive, but we were keen to try them. Without thinking, we spent all the money our mother had left for us on a small bag of Chinese sandwich cookies and a cup of sunflower seeds.

It would be more than a month before we saw our mother again.

Winter had arrived and the days got dark too quickly. The air was so cold that the door to our house kept freezing shut. And it was very difficult for us to figure out how to make a fire to heat the house and cook food. My mother had left us some firewood, but we weren't very good at chopping it into small pieces. The ax was too heavy for me and I had no gloves. For a long time I picked splinters out of my hands.

Early one evening, I was in charge of making the fire in the kitchen, but I used wet wood and it started to smoke too much. My sister and I were struggling to breathe, but we couldn't open the doors or windows because they were frozen solid. We screamed and banged on the wall to our neighbor's house, but nobody could hear us. I finally picked up the ax and broke the ice to open the door.

It was a miracle we survived that terrible month. The food my mother left for us ran out quickly, and by the end of December we were nearly starving. Sometimes our friends' mothers would feed us, but they were struggling, too. The famine was supposed to have ended in North Korea in the late 1990s, but life was still very hard, even years later. My father's younger sister who lived in Hyesan had nothing to spare, and my uncle Park Jin was furious that my father had brought more trouble and disgrace to the family by getting himself arrested. It was so hurtful because my parents had always been generous with him and his family. Now we didn't feel we could ask him for help.

Our neighbor Kim Jong Ae was a kind woman who tried to keep an eye on us. She was a party member and worked for the Military Mobilization Department so she was doing better than most people we knew. I'll never forget the freezing day when my sister and I were outside playing in the snow with our friends—it was winter break from school—and when we came back to our house at five p.m. it was already dark. We had no lights in the house and no food. We just sat in the kitchen, preparing for another cold, hungry night, when Jong Ae appeared in the doorway with a steaming bowl of rice. I can still close my eyes and remember the incredible aroma of that rice, probably the best thing I have ever smelled in my life. I have never had a more delicious meal, or been more grateful for a simple act of kindness.

My friend Yong Ja and her grandmother helped us, too. Yong Ja sometimes slept at our house so that my sister and I wouldn't be so afraid of the dark. It is painful to write these words because I don't like to remember how I felt during those desperate times. Since then I have hated the dark. Even now when I'm upset and having a hard time, I turn on all the lights and make the room as bright as possible. If night never came again, I would be happy.

To fill up the lonely hours, my sister and I would sing the same songs our mother soothed us with when we were babies. We wished we could just hear her voice telling us she would come back, but there were no phones and no number where we could reach her.

When my mother knocked on the door without warning one day in January, we couldn't believe it. We just threw our arms around her and wouldn't let go. All three of us cried and cried with happiness that we were all still alive. She brought us some rice and corn and dried beans, and we were so hungry it was hard to resist cooking ourselves a big feast. But we knew the food had to last because our mother told us she couldn't stay long. She had to get back to Pyongyang to earn some money, and to try to help our father.

The story she told us was terrifying: Soon after she arrived, she found he was being held at a detention and interrogation center called a *ku ryujang*. At first they wouldn't let her see my father, but finally she was able to bribe one of the guards to get in. My father was in a shocking condition. He told her the police had tortured him by beating one place on his leg until it swelled up so badly that he could barely move. He couldn't even get to the toilet. Then the guards tied him in a kneeling position with a wooden stick behind his knees, causing even more excruciating pain. They wanted to know how much he had sold to smugglers and who else was involved in the operation. But he told them very little.

Later he was moved to Camp 11, the Chungsan "reeducation" labor camp northwest of Pyongyang. This type of facility is mostly for petty criminals or women who have been captured escaping North Korea. But these kinds of prisons can be as brutal as the felony-level and even the political prison camps in the North Korean gulag. In "reeducation" camps, the inmates are forced to work at hard labor all day, in the fields or in manufacturing jobs, on so little food that they have to fight over scraps and sometimes eat rats to survive. Then they have to spend the evenings memorizing the Leaders' speeches or engaging in endless self-criticism sessions. Although they have committed "crimes against the people," these prisoners are thought to be redeemable, so they can be sent back to society once they have repented and finished an intensive refresher course in Kim Il Sung's teachings. Sometimes prisoners are given a trial, sometimes not. But my mother thought it was a good sign that my father had been sent to one of these so-called lighter facilities. It gave her hope that we could all be together again soon.

Eunmi and I were relieved to have our mother home. That night we all snuggled together by the fire, and I slept without fear for the first time in weeks. The next day, though, we woke up to detectives pounding on our door. They had come to arrest my mother for questioning about my father's crimes. But when the police officers saw that she had young children in the house, they took pity on us. They asked if she had any relatives who could take us while she was being interrogated, and she told them about my father's brother, Uncle Jin. So the police asked the head of our *inminban* to find him and bring him to our house. When he arrived, they ordered him to care for us while our mother was being questioned, and then they led her away.

For the next few days, she had to sit in a room at the prosecutors' office in Hyesan day and night, writing statements about herself and my father and everything they had done wrong. Then a detective would read the pages and ask her more questions. At night they would simply lock the office door and go away. In the morning they came back to start the interrogation again.

Finally, she was released. The police trusted her enough to travel, but she was told she had to return to continue her interrogation at a later time.

Eunmi and I were so grateful that she wasn't sent away to prison, like our father. But when she came to see us at Uncle Jin's house, we begged her to let us stay at home while she returned to Pyongyang to try to help my father. My uncle and aunt were unkind to us; they ordered us around like servants, and made us feel so unwelcome that we didn't know what might happen to us when she was gone. We told our mother we were better off staying alone in our own house. Besides, we were learning how to take care of ourselves. She reluctantly agreed.

I still cry whenever I think of the moment my mother left us again. She was wearing a beige-colored jacket, and I was crying and holding on to it, not letting her go. Life without her was so difficult. I wanted to live like other kids, with someone to wait for me to come home, to tell me it's time for dinner or it's time to wake up. I just missed her so much. At first she tried to pretend it wasn't a big deal that she was leaving again, but then she started crying with me, too.

"Please be a good girl, Yeonmi-ya," she said. "You just have to sleep for forty nights and I'll be home."

That felt like a very long time to me, and it was. My mother would come and go frequently over the next seven months. Often she would be gone for several weeks at a time. She had a business buying and selling watches, clothes, and used televisions—all things that the government didn't care much about if they caught you. But it took a long time to move all her products. She was able to see my father only once more, and neither of them had any way of knowing how long he would be held in prison. Sometimes when she came back to Hyesan she had no food or snacks to bring us. When we were younger, my sister and I might have complained, but not anymore. All we cared about was that she was all right, and that we were together at least for a while.

M eanwhile, my sister and I had to drop out of school. Education is supposed to be free in North Korea, but students have to pay for their own supplies and uniforms, and the school expects you to bring gifts of food and other items for the teachers. We no longer had money for these things, so nobody cared if we went to class or not. Besides, Eunmi and I had to spend all of our time just staying alive.

To wash our clothes and dishes we had to walk down to the river and break the ice. Every day or so, one of us had to stand in line for tap water for cooking and drinking. The food our mother left with us never lasted very long, so we were very hungry and skinny.

As our mother predicted, the children in town started mocking us because we were a family of criminals. Everybody was saying my father had destroyed our bright future and left us in a hopeless situation. We put our chins in the air and walked away from these people. But we knew they were telling the truth. Once my father became a prisoner and was kicked out of the Workers' Party, our destiny was irreversible. There was little hope we would ever be a happy family again.

A fter that long, dark winter of hunger in 2002 and 2003, I got a painful rash on my face that cracked and bled when I went out in the sun. I was dizzy most of the time and had a bad stomach. A lot of other children suffered from the same thing, and I later found out we all had pellagra, which is caused by a lack of niacin and other minerals. A starvation diet of mostly corn and no meat will bring on the disease, which can kill you in a few years unless you get better nutrition.

After I escaped to South Korea, I was surprised to hear that the blossoms and green shoots of spring symbolize life and renewal in other parts in the world. In North Korea, spring is the season of death. It is the time of year when our stores of food are gone, but the farms produce nothing to eat because new crops are just being planted. Spring is when most people died of starvation. My sister and I often heard the adults who saw dead bodies on the street make clucking noises and say, "It's too bad they couldn't hold on until summer."

Now when I travel to places like America and England in April and May, I have the luxury of enjoying nature and drinking in the beauty of spring flowers. But I also remember the time when I cursed the bright green hills and wished those flowers were made of bread or candy.

The only good thing about spring was that we didn't need as much wood to burn, and we could walk to the small mountains outside of town where we could fill our bellies with bugs and wild plants so that the hunger didn't bite so sharply. Some of the plants even tasted good, like wild clover flowers. Eunmi's favorite was something we called "cat plant," which had small, soft green leaves. We also chewed on certain roots without swallowing them, just to feel like we were putting something in our mouths. But one time we chewed on a root that made our tongues swell up so we couldn't talk for at least an hour. After that we were more careful.

Lots of children like to chase after dragonflies; when I caught them, I ate them.

The boys in our neighborhood had a plastic cigarette lighter, and they taught me how to cook a dragonfly head on an open flame. It gave off an incredible smell like roasted meat, and it tasted delicious. Later in the summer, we roasted cicadas, which were considered a gourmet treat. My sister and I would sometimes spend all day up there in the fields, trying to eat as much as we could before returning to our quiet dark house.

In late August 2003, my mother came back to Hyesan and told us to pack up a few things we would need. Her interrogation was finished, and she couldn't leave us alone for another winter. Our mother sold our house so that we could have money to move back to her hometown of Kowon. But it was a tricky thing to buy and sell property in North Korea because everything belonged to the state. Because it was illegal, the sale of our house was never recorded and there were no deeds or other papers to sign. My mother and the buyer just made an oral agreement, and trusted that nobody would inform on them.

We were leaving the only home we had ever known.

Eight

A Song for Chosun

My mother dropped us off to stay with her brother, my father's old friend Min Sik, who lived with his wife and two sons in the family house that now belonged to him. Min Sik had a job driving for a collective car service that provided transportation for local factories. But nobody in North Korea could live on their wages alone. In 2002, an average worker's salary was about 2,400 won per month, worth about $2 at the unofficial exchange rate. That couldn't even buy ten pounds of cheap grain, and prices kept going up. My uncle couldn't afford to feed two more children.

But my mother had money from the house sale, which she used to lease a stall in the market for Min Sik's wife to help support the family. The government was now regulating the *jangmadang*s and charging fees for spots in the covered markets—and taking bribes for the best positions. My uncle's wife started a business selling fish and rice cakes, but it wasn't very profitable. My mother gave what money was left to her brother to hold, but he ran through it quickly.

Soon after we arrived, my mother's big sister, Min Hee, came to Kowon to visit her brother. She felt bad when she saw how we were struggling, and when she returned to her village of Songnam-ri deep in the countryside, she took me home with her. Her husband was a retired government official, and their children were grown, so she decided I would not be much of a burden.

My aunt's house was built in the traditional style, with a thatched roof and wooden beams. In front was a swept clay courtyard, with a round brick chimney and fireplace for outdoor cooking. Aunt Min Hee and her husband were very kind to me, but I was lonely without my sister and my mother and often cried. It took time for me to adapt to country life.

There was rarely electricity in the village, so nobody relied on it, and they lived as they had before the technology even existed. At night we traveled by moonlight or just starlight. A lot of women wore traditional skirts as everyday clothes. The mountains were all around us, with springs so clean and pure you could just dip your hand into one to drink. The fanciest transportation available was an oxcart.

Not many houses had clocks in Songnam-ri, so we would wake up whenever the rooster crowed. Most of the time the roosters were very accurate, but sometimes they were not, so many people's schedules were messed up when the roosters failed to crow. My aunt had lots of chickens, and it was my job to watch the hens lay their eggs and to make sure the other chickens didn't eat them and that nobody came by to steal them.

I also had other work washing dishes and hauling wood from the forest, but I didn't mind at all. Besides, I wasn't weak from hunger anymore. In fact, I had starved for so long that I couldn't stop eating. I was like a baby bird: whenever I opened my eyes, my mouth opened at the same time; whenever I closed my eyes, my mouth closed, too. My aunt cooked good and simple food for me, dishes made from corn and potatoes and pepper plants she grew in her garden. She also grew sweet potatoes to sell in the market, but we would keep the leaves for ourselves to eat. They were very nutritious. The pigs ate what we left on our plates. The house also had a vineyard around it and I tasted grapes for the first time. It was like heaven.

I recovered very quickly and gained back the weight I had lost. I even started to grow. I'm not very tall now, but I think that if I'd had enough to eat all my life and didn't have to carry so many buckets of water on my head, I would be a lot taller!

My aunt's grown daughter was a doctor who went to medical school in Hamhung. While I was living with my aunt, my cousin was practicing obstetrics and gynecology at Songnam-ri's hospital. She was also engaged to a local policeman in an arranged marriage. I liked him because he brought home videos to watch that the police had confiscated in raids.

Even though my cousin was supposed to be healing people in the hospital, the government didn't supply her or any of the doctors with medicines. In the cities, patients can sometimes buy their own drugs on the black market, but in the rural areas, that isn't always possible. In Songnam-ri, the nearest *jangmadang* was more than five miles away and there was no direct route to get there. People had to walk over a mountain and across a river and a stream—even the oxcart couldn't make it all the way. This left so many people helpless in emergency situations. The government encouraged everyone to be resourceful, even doctors, as part of the *juche* policy of self-reliance, so the doctors would make their own traditional medicines to have on hand. My cousin often took me with her into the mountains to search for plants, tree barks, and nuts to use for different treatments. I followed along like a happy puppy, learning what is useful, what is edible, what is poisonous.

The doctors in Songnam-ri had to be farmers, too. They culti-

vated medicinal plants, and actually grew their own cotton to have a
supply of bandages and dressings. But there were always shortages of
everything. Even in big city hospitals there is no such thing as "disposable" supplies. Bandages are washed and reused. Nurses go from room
to room using the same syringe on every patient. They know this is
dangerous, but they have no choice. When I came to South Korea, I
was amazed when the doctors threw away the tools they had just used
on me.

Even while I was living there, I couldn't help feeling a strange
nostalgia for the simpler way of life in Songnam-ri. I don't know
how else to explain it, but all these new experiences seemed deeply
familiar. Up in the mountains, surrounded by nature, I felt closer to
my real self than at any time I have known. In some ways it was like
living in ancient Chosun, the long-ago Korean kingdom I had heard
about from my little grandmother in Kowon. I think she had the same
yearning for a place neither of us had known, that existed only in old
songs and dreams.

The year I spent in the country gave me a safe place to rest and
heal. But it was not my fate to stay there forever. One day in early
2004, my mother visited with some terrible news. My father had been
convicted in a secret trial and sentenced to hard labor at a felony-level
prison camp. We thought that he was sentenced to seventeen years,
but later found out it was ten. No matter, because hardly anyone survived very long in these places. Everybody knew this, because the
regime wanted us to fear these camps. They were places where you
are no longer considered a human being. Prisoners in these camps
can't even look directly at the guards, because an animal cannot look
a human in the face. They normally aren't allowed visits from family;

they can't even write letters. Their days are spent in bone-breaking labor with only thin porridge to eat, so they are always weak and hungry. At night the prisoners are crammed into small cells and forced to sleep like packed fish, head to toe. Only the strongest live long enough to serve out their sentences.

A chill washed through my veins when I realized that I might never see my father again. And even if he were to survive, when he got out I would be a grown woman. Would we even know each other?

M y mother wanted us to be together again, so she took me back with her to Kowon and persuaded her brother to let the three of us stay with him. She would earn enough to support us.

My mother, Eunmi, and I moved into a small room attached to the main house. It had a very tiny bed with a wire platform. We put some boards on it, but that made it too hard, and it was still very shaky. So we took it out and slept together on the floor. Outside the door there was a tiny open kitchen under a small roof, where water would drip into pans when it rained. Later my uncle and some of his friends built a wall for us so that we could keep the fire going. We lived there for the next two years.

Kowon was a much smaller city than Hyesan, and the people were much friendlier. There also seemed to be fewer thieves. Hyesan suffered from a lot of crime once the economy collapsed, and we had to hide our property behind locked doors. We dried our clothes inside the house, because anything we left on the line would be taken. People would take everything, even your dogs. In North Korea, people have dogs for two reasons: one is for keeping your home safe, and the other is for food. As in many places in Asia, dog meat is a delicacy where I grew up, although I loved dogs too much to want to eat them.

Our dogs had to be chained outside during the day and locked in the house at night or someone would steal them to sell, or cook them for dinner.

Kowon was a little safer, but the people there were also desperately poor. The main difference in Kowon was that everybody still shared with one another the way they had in the old times. In Hyesan, we might make rice cakes and secretly eat them by ourselves, or share only with very close neighbors. But in Kowon, if you had rice cakes, all the neighbors would show up and eat until there was nothing left for you. You had no choice.

My aunt in Kowon was very loyal to the regime and was the head of her *inminban*. *Inminban* meetings were held once a week as a way for the state to keep track of everybody's activities and announce new directives. On Saturdays, we would all meet for propaganda and self-criticism sessions. These were organized around student and work units, with students reporting to their classrooms and workers to their offices.

We began by writing out quotations from Kim Il Sung or Kim Jong Il, the way people in other parts of the world would copy Bible verses or passages from the Koran. Next you had to write down everything you had done in the previous week. Then it was time to stand up in front of the group to criticize yourself. At a typical session I might begin, "This week, I was too spoiled and not thankful enough for my benevolent Dear Leader's eternal and unconditional love." I would add that I had not worked diligently enough to fulfill the mission that the party ordered us to do, or did not study hard enough, or did not love my comrades enough. This last one was very important, because we were all comrades in the journey to fight against "American bastards," or "insane Western wolves." I would conclude, "Since then, our Dear Leader has forgiven me because of his benevolent, gracious leadership. I thank him, and I will do better next week."

After we had finished our public confessions, it was time to criticize others. I would always jump up and volunteer. I was really good at it. Usually I would pick one classmate who would then have to stand up and listen intently while I listed his or her transgressions: He was not following what our Leader taught us. Or she was not participating in the group mission. When I was finished, my victim would have to thank me and assure everyone that he or she would correct the behavior. Eventually it was my turn to be criticized. I hated it, of course, but I would never let it show in my face.

The self-criticism meetings in Hyesan could be intense, but the ones in Kowon were brutal. The people in this very isolated and patriotic part of the country really thought of themselves as revolutionaries. Their devotion to the regime hadn't been compromised with too much exposure to the world beyond the borders. And the authorities seemed determined to keep it that way as long as they could.

I was almost ten years old now, and my mother enrolled me in the local middle school, even though I had skipped the last two years of elementary school. I found the course work bewildering. And the schools in Kowon were much more rigid than the ones I had attended in Hyesan. Here the children were never allowed to do anything alone. In the morning, after we finished our collective labor cleaning the streets or polishing the monuments, the schoolchildren were expected to line up and march to class. We would swing our arms in unison, singing cheerful songs with lyrics like, "How bright is our socialist country! We are the new generation!" We usually did the same thing going home at the end of a day of study.

In North Korea, schoolchildren do more than study. They are part of the unpaid labor force that keeps the country from total collapse. I always had to carry a set of work clothes in my school bag, for the afternoons when they marched us off for manual labor. In the spring we helped the collective farms with their planting. Our job was to carry stones to clear the fields, put in the corn, and haul water. In June and July we weeded the fields, and in fall we were sent out to pick up the rice or corn or beans that had been missed by the harvesters. Our small fingers were good for this purpose. I hated this work. But we were told we couldn't waste a single grain when people were hungry.

The only time I was happy in the fields was when I found a mouse hole, because mice were doing the same kind of work. You could dig up their homes and find a couple of pounds of corn or beans they were storing for later. If we were lucky, we would catch the mice, too. But all the grain we gleaned from the fields belonged to the school, not us. At the end of the day, the teachers collected whatever we found. They didn't want us to take any grain for ourselves, so they would line us up and say, "Show us your pockets!" We learned to put our work clothes over our school clothes so we could hide some grain in the bottom layer and bring it home to eat.

One of the big problems in North Korea was a fertilizer shortage. When the economy collapsed in the 1990s, the Soviet Union stopped sending fertilizer to us and our own factories stopped producing it. Whatever was donated from other countries couldn't get to the farms because the transportation system had also broken down. This led to crop failures that made the famine even worse. So the government came up with a campaign to fill the fertilizer gap with a local and renewable source: human and animal waste. Every worker and schoolchild had a quota to fill. You can imagine what kind of problems this created for our families. Every member of the household had a daily assignment, so when we got up in the morning, it was like a war. My aunts were the most competitive.

"Remember not to poop in school!" my aunt in Kowon told me every day. "Wait to do it here!"

Whenever my aunt in Songnam-ri traveled away from home and had to poop somewhere else, she loudly complained that she didn't have a plastic bag with her to save it. "Next time I'll remember!" she would say. Thankfully, she never actually did this.

The big effort to collect waste peaked in January, so it could be ready for growing season. Our bathrooms in North Korea were usually far away from the house, so you had to be careful that the neighbors didn't steal from you at night. Some people would lock up their outhouses to keep the poop thieves away. At school the teachers would send us out into the streets to find poop and carry it back to class. So if we saw a dog pooping in the street, it was like gold. My uncle in Kowon had a big dog who made a big poop—and everyone in the family would fight over it. This is not something you see every day in the West.

My mother worked at all kinds of jobs in Kowon. She did facial massages and eyebrow tattoos for women. She bought and sold videocassettes and televisions on the black market. It still wasn't enough to keep us fed with rice. Once again my sister and I would go to the countryside to look for wild plants and insects to fill our stomachs. I loved the sweet white flowers of the false acacia tree that grew wild in the mountains. But the best thing to find was grasshoppers. My motor skills had improved as I got older, and I was really good at catching them. When my mother fried them, they were delicious to eat.

Most wild foods, though, were not so good for humans. They were just to fill you up. When I walked in the hills, I would pluck lots of different leaves—some for me, and some for the rabbits we kept back in town. They were my good friends; we would share meals together. Even now when I go for a walk I can tell which kind of plant is the rabbits' favorite. But I still don't like salad very much because it reminds me of those hard times.

When I was living in Kowon, I raised the rabbits from babies and gave them names like Red Eye, Blackie, and Goldie. But they could not be pets because when the time came, we skinned and ate them. Most of the time, it was the only meat we had. The pelts were very valuable, too. In North Korea, all the schools had to collect rabbit fur for the soldiers' winter uniforms. Every student had to bring five pelts each semester. But it's difficult to tan your own rabbit leather, and the military had high standards, so the school would often reject the bad ones. The only way to be sure you could fill your quota was to buy expertly tanned skins in the *jangmadang*. Of course, the school administrators didn't give all the rabbit furs to the military—they kept them for themselves to make some money. I know this because my mother had a business buying and selling rabbit furs. In fact, sometimes she would buy pelts from the school that she had just sold to customers looking to fill their quotas.

This insane system was good for my mother, but hard on everybody else.

When I was about eleven years old, I began to follow in my parents' footsteps. My mother gave me some seed money to start my own business. I used the loan to buy some rice vodka to bribe the guard at a state-owned orchard that grew persimmons. He let me and my sister sneak in and pick the fruit. We filled a big metal bucket and carried the persimmons for miles back to Kowon, where I sold them in the *jangmadang*.

"These are the most delicious persimmons!" I cried out to the cus-

tomers as they walked by. "Buy them here!" At the end of the day, I
had enough money to pay back my mother, buy some candy, and purchase another bottle to bribe the orchard guard. My sister picked fruit
with me until my mother put a stop to our little business venture: we
were wearing out our shoes too quickly walking to the orchard, and
she couldn't afford to buy new ones.

Still, I learned something important from my short time as a market vendor: once you start trading for yourself, you start thinking for
yourself. Before the public distribution system collapsed, the government alone decided who would survive and who would starve. The
markets took away the government's control. My small market trans-
actions made me realize that I had some control over my own fate. It
gave me another tiny taste of freedom.

Nine

Jangmadang Generation

I n the fall of 2005, my mother had to go into hiding: the police in Kowon were looking her.

In North Korea, you can't just choose where you want to live. The government has to give you permission to move outside your assigned district, and the authorities don't make it easy. The only good reasons are a job transfer, marriage, or divorce. Even though she was born and raised in the house her brother Min Sik now owned, my mother's official residence was still in Hyesan. Illegally changing your residence doesn't really matter for children, but for a grown-up like my mother, it was a big problem.

She had managed to stay out of trouble for a long time because my uncle was a party member and his wife was head of her *inminban*, so they had good connections with the local authorities. Once in a while the police would visit the house and ask my mother to stop by the station, which was a strong hint that they wanted a bribe to ignore her situation. But my mother was very busy and didn't pay enough attention to their signals. The police waited patiently for a long time, but they finally decided to send her to a reeducation camp for punishment. When she found out the police were looking for her, my mother ran away to stay with some friends. And that is why she was not home on the sunny afternoon when my father showed up at my uncle's door.

Eunmi was at school, and I was alone in our little room when I heard the dog barking loudly. Then I heard the sound of a man's voice talking to my uncle. My heart started pounding because the voice sounded familiar, but I wouldn't let myself believe it was my father. He had been in prison for almost three years, and I never expected to see him again. Then I heard my uncle calling, "Yeonmi-ya! Yeonmi-ya! Your father is here!"

I came running into the main house, and there was a stranger sitting with my uncle.

"Abuji?" I whispered. "Father?"

I hadn't allowed myself to speak that word in a long time, and it felt strange on my tongue. I took a closer look and it really was my father, but he was extremely skinny, and they had shaved off all his hair in prison. I always thought he was the biggest man in the world, my hero who could do everything. But now he seemed so tiny. Worse, his voice was so fearful and quiet I could hardly recognize it. I stood in front of him as he touched my face and hair, like a blind person reading a book, saying, "Is this really Yeonmi? Is this really Yeonmi?"

He didn't cry, he just looked at me. I wasn't a baby anymore. Now I was a young girl of twelve, almost an adolescent. "Is this really you, my daughter?"

I wanted to jump into his arms and hug him, but I was living under my uncle's roof, and I was afraid to show him how happy I was to see my father. My uncle, once my father's good friend, hated my father now, and often said terrible things about him. He blamed him for being irresponsible and getting arrested, leaving others with the burden of his wife and children. I was so sad that people who had been so respectful of my father when he was wealthy and powerful now treated him so badly. After a while, I couldn't stop myself and I threw my arms around my father and held on tight, afraid to ever let him go again.

After my father was arrested, I had stopped acting like a child. Now that he was back, I spent every moment I could snuggled in his lap, just like when I was a baby. And I wanted to do the same things we did when I was little. I used to sit on my father's knees and get bounced like a horse. I wanted to do that again, and even asked him to give me an airplane ride on his feet. My poor father tried to do it, but he put me down quickly, saying, "Ouch! My little puppy has really gotten big!" That was one of my nicknames as a small child. It made me cry to hear him say it again.

When Eunmi came home from school, we sent for my mother with word that my father was out of prison. He told us that he had gotten very sick, and he had bribed the warden to let him out on temporary leave.

We were shocked by my father's condition when we helped him change his clothes. You could see the bones under his flesh and his skin was coming off in sheets from malnutrition. My mother told me to run and buy some tofu water to bathe him and help heal his wounds. He was so hungry he wanted to eat everything, but his system couldn't take it after starving for so long. So she had to control him and make sure he ate only a little rice at a time or he would get sick.

When he was well enough to talk, he told her what had happened.

The warden knew my father was in prison for a big financial crime, and my father convinced him that he had hidden some money with a woman in Hyesan. If the warden would let my father out for sick leave, he promised he would give him one million North Korean won. That was a huge bribe, enough money to buy a fine house. The warden was greedy enough to believe him, but my father never in-tended to pay him, even if he'd had the money. He figured that once he got out of prison for medical reasons, they couldn't suddenly drag him back without exposing their own corruption. It might be possi-ble, after a while, for them to say my father had recovered enough to return to prison. But he would worry about that some other time.

My father persuaded the warden to allow him to visit his family in Kowon before traveling to Hyesan. There he would be released to his brother, Park Jin, to help him get treatment for the worsening pain in his stomach. The warden sent a prison doctor to travel with him, supposedly to escort him all the way to Hyesan. His real purpose, of course, was to collect the money. But he would not succeed, because there was no money to collect.

My father stayed in Kowon for a few days, and then left for Hye-san. Once he was settled there, he would send for us.

My mother, meanwhile, decided to turn herself in to the police and was sentenced to a month of reeducation at something called the "workers' training corps," which was like a mobile slave labor camp. The prisoners slept together in a lice-infested room and were sent out during the day to build bridges and work on other heavy construction projects. There were only a few women in my mother's unit, but the guards made them work as hard as the men. If anyone was too slow, the whole group would be forced to run around the camp all night without any sleep as punishment. To make sure that didn't happen, the prisoners would beat one another if someone wasn't working fast enough. The guards didn't have to do a thing. And the pace was so grueling that some prisoners were near death after a few weeks in the camps. When my mother started her sentence, it was nearing the end of fall, and she suffered in the cold with a thin jacket and no gloves.

Sometimes the construction sites were far away, but when my mother was closer to Kowon, my sister and I visited her in the field.

The first time we went, my sister and I woke up at five o'clock in the morning to cook for her. We knew the prisoners were never given enough to eat. I cooked a small pumpkin and mixed it with rice and corn, then I sliced some radishes and cured them with salt. Salted radishes are the poor person's kimchi; we couldn't afford the ingredients necessary to make the spicy sauce for the traditional pickled cabbage.

We started walking at six a.m., when it was still dark, but we took a wrong turn on the way to the construction site. As we walked, we became so hungry that we started tasting the food we had brought with us. By the time we got to the work site, we had eaten all of it. We both felt bad arriving with nothing to offer, but my mother was so happy to see us. She was still our mother and more concerned about us than herself, so she brought us some water to drink. The guards gave her only a few moments to visit with us, so we visited as often as possible, bringing food with us when we could.

Thankfully, my mother's term at the workers' training corps was short. She managed to bribe someone at the police station and was released after only sixteen days. After resting with us for a short time, she took the train to Hyesan to visit my father. She knew the police would hound her as long as her residence was in Hyesan—and the only way to change it while he was alive was to divorce my father. They still loved each other, but they secretly agreed that a divorce was the only practical solution. If he had to go back to prison, Kowon would be a better place for the family to live, because it was warmer and cheaper than Hyesan. So they acted quickly, and the divorce was recorded in April 2006.

Meanwhile, a friend of my father's gave him a place to live rent free until he could pay him back. He had plans to revive his business with my mother's help. At least for now, he wanted us to move back to Hyesan to be with him. In May, I took the train north by myself to live with my father; Eunmi and my mother joined us a few months later. We were finally together again.

My father's apartment was on the top floor of an eight-story building in the suburb of Wiyeon, a few miles east of our old neighborhood in Hyesan. The apartment overlooked the Yalu River, and you could see China from the window. There were three rooms, which we shared with two other families. The walls were thin, so we had to speak very softly or everyone could hear our business. Because there was no elevator in the building, we had to walk up eight flights in a dark stairwell to get to the apartment—that's why in North Korea the lower-floor apartments are more desirable. The less money you have, the higher up you live.

My father was receiving medical treatment for his stomach problems, but once again, none of the doctors could find out what was wrong with him. He was in a real dilemma, because he was too sick to work, but if he got healthy again, they would send him back to prison. Instead he lived in a kind of limbo. His ID card had been destroyed when he went to prison—only human beings can have IDs and he was considered subhuman. Without the card, you can't go anywhere, so it made it impossible for him to travel around buying metal to sell to the smugglers. Besides, he constantly had to check in with the police, who were keeping a close eye on him. So he stayed home and cared for me and my sister while my mother took over the business.

The same man who offered my father the apartment was willing to invest some start-up money in a business venture my mother proposed. She and the man's son traveled to a place near Songnam-ri to buy silver, then they came back to Hyesan and sold it to smugglers. My parents made a small profit from these deals, but we were still very poor. Often our only food was black frozen potatoes, which made my father even sicker.

I had missed Hyesan so much after we moved away, and I couldn't wait to see all my friends again. Yong Ja had grown so big and tall—at least for a North Korean. She had always been a strong girl, but now she was taking Tae Kwan Do lessons that made her even tougher. It made me feel safe to spend time with her, because so much of Hyesan had changed in the three years I'd been away. The city seemed livelier and more prosperous now, because of the legal and illegal trade with China. And the young people looked and acted so different. Older girls straightened their wavy hair with a cream called "Magic" that was smuggled across the border. Some were even dyeing their hair and wearing jeans, which was illegal. Jeans were symbols of American decadence, and if the police caught you wearing them they would take scissors and cut them up. Then you could be sentenced to a day of reeducation or a week of extra work. But it didn't stop the teenagers from trying new things.

Yong Ja explained to me that all the teenagers were now "dating"—which was really just boys and girls hanging out together. But it seemed incredibly strange to me. Even kindergarten students were pretending to have boyfriends and girlfriends. She warned me about some of the new rules between the sexes. For instance, if a boy made a popping or clucking sound with his mouth when you walked by, you shouldn't turn around and look at him unless you were interested in dating him. If you did, he would never leave you alone. I made this mistake a few times because I was so confused by these new customs. In fact, I felt like a country bumpkin. Yong Ja even laughed at me for the Kowon accent I had picked up while I was away. The people in the interior of North Korea speak much more slowly than residents of the

Chinese border towns. Arriving from Kowon was like an American from Atlanta moving to New York City. It took a while for me to sound like a native again.

I enrolled in middle school in Wiyeon and made a new group of friends, mostly girls who were a few years older than me. Again I had skipped a few grades, and was falling far behind in school. When Eunmi arrived from Kowon, she was fifteen years old and further along in her schooling. She quickly made lots of her own friends and we didn't hang out with each other as often as before. She also started dating for the first time, and fell for a boy whose father was from China. My mother urged her to break up with him because he was from such a poor *songbun*, even worse than ours. Eunmi did as she was asked, but it caused some friction in our family.

My new friends knew all about the latest fashions from watching South Korean soap operas and international music videos. Nobody had home computers, and there was, of course, no connection to the Internet to download illegal foreign media. Instead it was smuggled across the river from China every night. Thin DVDs had replaced bulky cassettes, making it easier to bring more of them into the country. What had been a trickle just a few years ago was now a flood.

Some of my friends had rooms with thick curtains they could use for watching DVDs, so we could play movies and dance around to the soundtracks. We also listened to music tapes and CDs—anything we could get our hands on. My sister and I liked the sad love songs best. Our favorite was about two people who made an oath to be true to each other by crossing their pinky fingers. Then one of them was suddenly gone. It always made us cry.

If it wasn't for those foreign DVDs and CDs, we wouldn't have known any songs except for the ones we were taught about Kim Il Sung and Kim Jong Il. We would try to change those to make them more interesting. One of the older boys we hung out with played the guitar, and when we sang along with him, we would leave out the parts about the Kims. Whenever I sang those songs, I felt more free. It was lucky we didn't get caught. But we were young and didn't think about the future.

North Koreans my age and younger are sometimes called the *Jang-madang* Generation, because we grew up with markets, and we couldn't remember a time when the state provided for everyone's needs. We didn't have the same blind loyalty to the regime that was felt by our parents' generation. Still, while the market economy and outside media weakened our dependence on the state, I couldn't make the mental leap to see the foreign movies and soap operas I loved to watch as models for a life I could lead.

I was about to become a teenager, and was beginning to be curious about romance. My girlfriends and I fantasized about the couples we saw in those movies, who looked into each other's eyes and spoke with such soft, beautiful accents. We tried to imitate them, and when boys would ask us out, we made them speak like South Koreans. Of course, "going out" in North Korea was much more innocent than even the tamest scenes we watched. I had seen romance only in the movies, and I had no idea what Pretty Woman was doing when the camera looked away. We were still completely innocent. All I cared about in *Pretty Woman* were the beautiful clothes that Yong Ja and I tried to re-create for our paper dolls.

It's so embarrassing to say, but I never knew kissing was meant to be romantic. Because my mother and father gave me lots of kisses when I was young, I thought it was something everybody did to show affection. There is no such thing as sex education in North Korea. Maybe mothers or doctors talked about sex with a girl before her wedding day, but I never heard about that. Several times, as a child, I had asked my mother how I was born, but she only told me that I would find out when I grew up. The boys, I think, were just as innocent as the girls.

In Hyesan, it was still rare to have your own landline telephone, and only the wealthiest had cell phones. The only way for a boy to make a date with a girl he liked was to go find her. Of course, parents didn't want their daughters meeting with boys. That generation still thought dating was scandalous, so the boys had to find ways to get past the barricades. I knew a few boys who wanted to date me, and each tried climbing the stairs to our eighth-floor apartment and knocking on the door.

My mother would get upset and yell through the closed door, "Get out! Go away!" She wouldn't let me out. To get around her, the boys gave me a signal in school, and in the evening they would come by and stand outside the building, shouting the code name so that I could hear it and make an excuse to come down. Of course, my sister also had boys wanting to date her. And there were lots of other teenage girls in the apartment building, so after sunset it got very noisy out there.

I was never really interested in dating anyone until I met Chun Guen, my first love. At eighteen, he was five years older than me, and he was in his final year at a special high school for the brightest students in all of Ryanggang province. He was taller than most Korean men, with pale skin and a quiet voice. We ran into each other while I was visiting some family friends who lived in his building, next to ours. At first Chun Guen would just nod or say hello as we were passing in the hallway or on the street. Then one day he asked me out. I really wanted to go out with him, but I had to refuse. I knew that our story could only have a sad ending.

Because my family was new in that part of town, Chun Guen didn't know that I was the daughter of a criminal. He came from a very wealthy and powerful family. His father had studied abroad and earned a PhD and was now a distinguished professor of agriculture at the university. His mother was a very important political person with a high rank in the Workers' Party. If his parents were to find out that we were together, he would be in big trouble. And if he were to get serious about me or marry me, it would destroy his life. Chun Guen would never be able to join the Workers' Party, never get to study at the best universities and have a distinguished career. I would be like a wound, a burden to drag him down. So I kept telling him no.

But he was persistent. So one day I agreed to come up to a party at his apartment while his parents were out. It was an innocent thing. There were lots of older boys and girls from his school. I was the youngest, and definitely the poorest guest. Suddenly I became very aware of my shabby, secondhand clothes and the holes in my pants. In Korea, we take off our shoes before we enter someone's home, so everyone could see how many times I had mended my ugly socks. It was humiliating to see myself among all those rich kids.

Chun Guen's apartment seemed huge—the same size as ours, but for only one family instead of three. I was astonished to see orange peels and eggshells in the garbage. Eggs were such rare delicacies in my family; we ate them only for New Year's and special occasions. And oranges were such a luxury that I had never eaten a whole one in my life—just a small piece when my father brought one home when we were wealthy. Throwing out the peel was such a waste.

I tried to pretend that I belonged there, and that I understood what everybody was talking about. Chun Guen was trying to explain how he used a computer in school, and I nodded politely and smiled, even though I had never seen one. Ordinary schools in North Korea did not have such things. I was so embarrassed that I got upset with Chun Guen for no reason and left early. I ran all the way home.

I thought that was the end of it, but Chun Guen was very patient and forgiving. And whenever I saw him I felt a twinge in my chest that was not hunger. So I agreed to see him sometimes, but only if he agreed to keep it a secret. We had to wait until it was fully dark to meet; if any of the neighbors saw us together, it would be too dangerous for him. When we saw each other on the street, one of us would cross to the other side or go a different direction.

Chun Guen found out where I lived, and one night he came and knocked on my door. My parents were impressed: my mother thought he was so respectful, so generous and smart. My father asked me to invite him for dinner. But I said no. I didn't want him to see how poor we were—and I still hadn't told him my father was a prisoner. What was the point? I knew I could never marry a man like Chun Guen. There could be no happy future for me. I would never go to college and would probably end up as a poor farmer's wife, if I didn't starve to death first.

It was wintertime now, and things were getting truly desperate for my family. There was a problem with the old railroad system that relied on electric power to move the trains. The power grid in the north had become so weak that the train from Pyongyang had to stop before it got to Hyesan, then turn around. After a while it stopped coming at all. My parents were waiting and waiting, but it never came. Now the only way to bring the metal from Pyongyang was by car, and that was impossible. My parents had nothing to sell, and nobody would loan them more money. They were spending cash that had been set aside for the business, and soon even that would be gone.

Our apartment was always cold when the wind whipped off the river, and my father walked to the mountains every day to look for wood to keep us warm. He would eat the snow to fill himself up. My mother did whatever small business deals she could in order to buy a little corn or frozen potatoes. But now we were hungry all the time. I no longer dreamed of bread. All I wanted was to have something to eat for my next meal. Skipping a meal could literally mean death, so that became my biggest fear and obsession. You don't care how food tastes and you don't eat with pleasure. You eat only with an animal instinct to survive, unconsciously calculating how much longer each bite of food will keep your body going.

My parents couldn't sleep. They were afraid they might not wake up, and then their children would starve to death. Once again, as they lay awake at night, they wondered what they could do to keep us alive.

Ten

The Lights of China

My family's fortune had changed forever, and never did that seem clearer than during the Lunar New Year celebration at my uncle Park Jin's house in February 2007. When I was young, my father was the richest in his clan, and everybody came to enjoy the holidays at our house. But now my uncle was the wealthy one who hosted the parties. And instead of treating my father like a brother, he ordered him around like a servant. In fact, during the months that my father had lived with my aunt and uncle in Hyesan after getting out of prison, they had made him sweep and clean the house. The family blamed my father for ruining their lives. Their *songbun* status had never been very good in the first place, and now, because he was a convicted criminal, it was much worse. Even my cousins mistreated him in front of his family and former friends. At the New Year celebration, they wouldn't let him sit and talk with the neighbors who used to eat and drink at his table. It was an extraordinarily difficult evening, but my father accepted it with weary resignation.

Before he was arrested, my father had been a brilliant, funny, irreverent man. But even as a thirteen-year-old girl, I could tell that his time in the prison camp had broken his spirit. He couldn't look a policeman in the face, not even the ones who used to joke and drink with him at his table. My father used to love South Korean music; now he refused to listen to it. He was afraid someone might hear it and report him. He sang only one song after he came out of the camp, "Our Country Is Worthier Than My Life," with the lyrics "The green forest flutters in our land and mountains, and I didn't plant even one tree. . . ." He wasn't the same person I'd known as a child.

I was so grateful when the New Year's party was over and we could finally leave.

It was two and a half miles from my uncle's house to our apartment building. My father stayed behind while my mother and sister and I walked home by ourselves along the dark river, guided only by flashes of light from the fireworks in the sky over China. I lived in North Korea, the country where we were supposed to have nothing to envy, and all I felt was envy—desperate envy for the people on the other side of the river. I still didn't dare to think about *why* we couldn't have so many things in North Korea, but I knew that I wanted to go where there was light and food. It was like being drawn to a flame without thinking about why. I wish I'd known at the time what that light really meant to North Koreans like me. Following it would cost me my innocence and, for a while, my humanity.

Every New Year, Kim Jong Il gave a statement that we all had to memorize. In 2007, it was more of the same: the North Korean people were stronger, our enemies would be defeated, the economy was getting better. But we could no longer believe the propaganda because our lives were just getting worse. My parents finally could take no more. They knew their daughters had no future here, so they began to discuss a way out.

We knew a man who had gone to work in Russia. It was basically slave labor, but at least he was fed so he didn't starve. And he was able to save enough money to start a successful business when he came back. My father knew another man who was sent to Libya as part of a labor force that earned foreign currency for the regime. When he returned, he told us that his life in Libya was very lonely—for three years he didn't see his family. But he could eat. And sometimes he even ate chicken wings.

We were all so hungry we wanted to hear every detail. He said that the Libyans ate lots of chicken—which was astounding to us—but they don't usually eat the whole bird. They cut off the wings and sold them for so little even North Koreans could afford them. Libya sounded like paradise to us. My father had wanted to go abroad, and hoped he would find a way to make some money to send back to us. But he never took the opportunity, and now it was out of the question.

North Koreans have always been told that the rest of the world was an impure, disgusting, and dangerous place. Worst of all was South Korea, which was a human cesspool, no more than an impoverished colony of the American bastards we were all taught to hate and fear. My father had no desire to ever go to South Korea, but China was different. Maybe if we could find a way to get across the river, we might have a chance.

My parents discussed their options in voices so quiet not even a mouse could hear them. We still had some relatives living in China, but my parents had no way to get in touch with them. Maybe if we could make it across the border we could find them and ask for their help. We all knew they were rich over there. We had seen Chinese television and all the luxuries it advertised. We knew people who had visited China legally, including Uncle Park Jin, and they said the Chinese all had plenty to eat. There were also rumors that young North Korean women could easily find jobs in China. A number of teenage girls had dropped out of sight recently, and people were whispering that they had gone to China. Maybe Eunmi and I could find work, too. My mother had also heard that in China there were not enough children, and because my sister and I were still very young, we might find people who would adopt us.

But in a place without an Internet or an outside newspaper, it was impossible to get reliable information. If you asked too many questions, you could be reported. So we had no idea if any of these rumors were true. My parents knew the black market, but they sold the metal only to smugglers who brought it to China; they had no connections of their own on the other side of the border. Ordinary smugglers didn't trade in people. That was a much more dangerous operation. And surveillance was too tight to risk crossing the river alone. We would need a broker to bribe the border guards and guide us across. But where could we find one?

My parents asked Eunmi and me to see if we could discreetly ask around and find out how the other girls were getting into China. My father urged my mother to go with us, too, if she could find a way. He would stay behind, he said, because he didn't think he could find work across the river. And he was worried about the family he would leave behind in North Korea. When women escaped to China, the government didn't get all that upset about it, and their relatives were usually not punished. But if a man like my father was to defect, the government would be very hard on his brother and sisters and their families. They might lose their jobs as doctors and professors, or even be sent to prison. Even though my uncle had treated him so badly, my father still felt loyalty to his family.

Besides, he didn't think we would be very far away. "After you go to China and once you are doing great, come down to the river at New Year," he told us. "Go to the beach where we always swim and wash our clothes, and I will meet you there."

My sister and I started asking our friends if they knew anything, and I kept my ears open for any information. One day I overheard a strange story a woman from the neighborhood was telling her friends. She said she knew a young woman who crossed the river and started knocking on doors in Chaingbai. Some people let her in and gave her lots of delicious foods and some pretty new clothes. Then they told her they wanted her to marry their son. She was not happy with the arrangement and tried to come back to Hyesan the way she came. But this time she was captured and arrested by North Korean border guards. One of the neighbors remarked that the girl was stupid to reject such a generous offer.

I had no idea what she was talking about.

Looking back, I wonder how we all could have been so naïve. None of us even knew the concept of "human trafficking," and couldn't imagine anything so evil as selling other people. And we weren't really capable of critical thinking because we had been trained not to ask questions. I actually thought that if we could just cross that river without being arrested or shot by the soldiers, Eunmi and I would be okay. But then, when you are so hungry and desperate, you are willing to take any risk in order to live.

Even as we were planning our escape, I was still secretly seeing Chun Guen. Our relationship was so innocent, we had never even held hands. One night when my building was completely dark, we stood in the stairwell at the end of the hall where an open window looked over the river. As always, the lights from Chaingbai glowed in the distance. I was cold, so he draped his jacket over my shoulders and put his arms around me.

I asked him, "What would it be like living there in all that brightness?"

"I don't know," he said.

I couldn't tell him about our plans to go there. It didn't matter anyway, because I knew he was leaving to start his military service in April. Usually young men go into the army for ten years. But because his parents were so rich and powerful, it was arranged that he would have to serve for only two years. Then he would go to university. His brilliant future was already laid out for him, but he told me he wanted me to wait for him. My family was still new enough in the neighborhood that he hadn't heard about my bad background. "Eight years, Yeonmi-ya," he said. "Wait for me that long, and I'm going to marry you." He said he would find a way to come see me every month no matter what. It broke my heart to hear him. Suddenly those lights I had always longed for seemed so cruel to me.

The next morning, Chun Guen came by to pick me up for a trip to the *jangmadang* in Hyesan. It was bad weather, so he paid for a motorcycle taxi to take us. It was a little bit different from a regular motorcycle because it had four wheels and an open trunk in the back. We climbed into the trunk and covered up under a tarp to keep out the cold rain. When we arrived at the market, he told me to pick out any necklace that I liked. I chose a pendant in the shape of a key. He told me he was the owner of the key that would open my heart. I smiled at him, but inside my heart was like stone.

I could not find a broker to take us to China, but Eunmi thought she had found one. She didn't know the name yet, but she said we would have to go soon. Spring was coming, and the river would melt if we didn't leave quickly.

But before we could make a plan, I woke up one morning with a high fever. "What's wrong, my daughter?" I heard my mother's voice from far away. I was so sick I couldn't even open my eyes. Then I started throwing up. Before long I had broken out in big red splotches all over my body. I felt like I was going to die. We heard rumors that a bad virus had crossed into our country from China, but nobody knew what to do about it. My mother borrowed money to buy some medicine for me, but days passed and I wasn't getting better. I had a terrible pain in my stomach and I couldn't keep any food down. I was getting so skinny and weak I couldn't even walk. So they took me to the hospital.

After the doctors examined me, they decided that my appendix had to come out. Because of my father's experience as a young man, my parents believed it was the only way to save my life. Even though we were supposed to have free medical care, the doctors expected us to pay them for the surgery. It sounds harsh, but the government gave them almost nothing, and bribery was the only way for them to survive. Somehow my parents persuaded the doctors to perform the operation if we supplied them with the anesthetic and antibiotics they needed. My mother went back to our old neighborhood and borrowed 20,000 won (about enough to buy fifty pounds of rice) from Kim Jong Ae, the kind woman who had lived next door to us, then used the money to buy the drugs on the black market.

When the doctors opened my stomach, they discovered it wasn't my appendix after all, just badly inflamed intestines. They removed my appendix anyway, gave me a strong antibiotic, and began to close me up. But the small amount of anesthetic they gave me did not last long enough, and I woke up before the surgery was finished. I can't even describe the pain. They had to hold me down because I was screaming so much. I thought I would lose my mind, but they finished the surgery anyway. Later my mother brought me some painkillers and I finally passed out.

The next thing I remember I was in a hospital room, with my mother sitting next to me. The beds were all full, so they put me on a pallet on the floor. She was stroking my hand, and after a while I noticed there was a ring on my finger. It was gold colored with little glass jewels on the top.

"Where did this come from, *Umma*?" I asked groggily.

"Chun Guen was here when you were sleeping," she said. He had brought me some snacks and juice and the ring to surprise me after my operation. But I would not wake up. She said he held my hand for a while, then put the ring on my finger before he left.

Later he came back to check on me, and the first thing he did was look at my hand.

"It makes me happy to see you wearing that ring, Yeonmi-ya," he said.

I did my best to smile, and showed him how loose it was on my finger. "It's too big," I said.

"Then you'll have to get better and gain some weight."

He came back to visit me almost every day while I recovered, and I was always so happy to see him.

My mother remained at my bedside. Because we had no money to bribe them, the nurses ignored me. My mother had to do everything, from keeping my incision clean to giving me whatever food she could find. The hospital was poorly equipped and filthy. To use the bathroom I had to get up and cross an open courtyard to reach the outhouse. At first I was too weak to stand. But once I was well enough to walk to the bathroom, I discovered that the hospital used the courtyard to store the dead. The whole time I was staying there, several bodies were stacked like wood between my room and the outhouse. Even more horrible were the rats that feasted on them day and night. It was the most terrible sight I have ever seen. The first thing the rats eat are the eyes, because that is the softest part of a body. I can still see those hollow red eyes. They come to me in my nightmares and I wake up screaming.

My mother couldn't believe the hospital just left the bodies out there in the open.

"Why can't you take these people away and bury them!" she demanded when a nurse walked by.

The nurse shrugged. "The government won't come and collect the bodies until there are seven of them. That's only five," she said, then walked away.

My mother had fought to hold on to her belief that she lived in a good country. She was shocked and saddened to realize how corrupt and pitiless North Korea had become. Now she was even more convinced that she couldn't let her daughters grow up in such a place. We had to get out as soon as possible.

The doctors told us I had to stay in that hellish hospital for seven days before they could remove my stitches. By now it was nearly the end of March, and time was running out to cross the frozen river. But I was still too weak to travel.

On March 25, the day before I was due to be released, my sister came to visit the hospital while my mother was with me. She told us she couldn't wait anymore, so she had found a broker to take her to China. She was sixteen years old now, and starting to make her own decisions. Even though my mother pulled her aside and begged her to wait for me, Eunmi said, "No, I'm leaving tonight with my friend's sister. If I don't take this opportunity, there may not be another." To my mother, she acted like this trip to China was not such a big deal, that she would just visit a neighborhood on the other side and maybe come right back. My mother didn't think this sounded right, but she couldn't persuade her to stay.

Later that night, Eunmi showed up at the hospital again. "We couldn't go tonight," she said.

"See, it's not so easy to escape!" my mother said.

"You wait," said my sister. "We've made another appointment to go tomorrow night."

Eleven

Missing

The next day, my uncle borrowed a car to take me home from the hospital. My family was hoping the doctors would remove my stitches and release me, but they refused because we still owed them money. So I had to stay another night.

My sister dropped by later with her friend. Eunmi was dressed in thin black clothes, and her hair was tied back. When we told her that I still could not leave, she whispered to my mother, so the other patients couldn't hear, "I'm sorry. I'm going tonight."

My mother didn't believe she would make it on her own. She just said, "Yeah, okay. You'll be back." She didn't hug her or even say good-bye. It was something she would regret for many years. I still cry when I think about that night. We didn't know how desperate Eunmi was. My father had made me a special dish in which you scoop out a potato and fry it with oil and spices. It was a rare and expensive treat, but he was worried because I was so skinny and had not eaten anything solid for many days. So he made me this special meal and gave it to Eunmi to bring to me. But I was feeling too sick to eat that night.

"I'm just not hungry, sister," I said.

"Do you mind if I eat it, then?"

"No, please do," I said.

At that she sat down next to me and stuffed the potato cake into her mouth so fast it looked like somebody was trying to steal the food from her.

"That was delicious," she said a few seconds later. "Please don't tell Father I ate it!"

"I promise."

It's still so painful to think about that time. That's all any of us wanted: just to eat.

My mother stayed with me that night. When Eunmi did not return as before, we assumed she had just gone home to the apartment. But at five o'clock in the morning my father walked into my room and he was shaking.

"Where's Eunmi?" he said. "Is she here?"

"No!" said my mother. "She's not with you?"

"No," he said. "She never came home."

Eunmi was gone. My mother never thought she would go through with her plan alone, and now she blamed herself. She was so upset she could hardly catch her breath. My father was wringing his hands. What if Eunmi had fallen into the icy water and drowned? What if they never found her body? My parents told me they had to search for my sister immediately, so I had to check out of the hospital right away. They found the doctors and pleaded with them until they finally took out my stitches.

I was still too weak to walk, but Chun Guen had come by the night before and offered to pick me up if I was released. I was so happy when he brought a friend with a motorcycle. The friend waited outside and we were alone for a while in the hospital room. Chun Guen finally admitted that he knew all about my family. Some jealous girls who lived in his building found out he was visiting me in the hospital, and told him everything about my father's being a criminal. But Chun Guen said he didn't care. He still wanted me to marry him. He was such an optimistic person, and so confident that he would make me the happiest person in the world. I told him nothing, and just smiled. That seemed to be enough for him. Somehow in my desperation he was willing to offer me a little bit of warmth, light, and hope. I will always be grateful for that.

We walked out of the hospital together and his friend started up the motorcycle. Chun Guen held on to me tightly as his friend drove slowly all the way to my building. I couldn't make it up the stairs, so Chun Guen carried me up eight flights to my apartment. He was very gallant for the first few floors, then he started sweating.

"You seem to be gaining weight!" he said with a grin.

I just smiled because it hurt too much to laugh.

When we got to my door, I was still too ashamed to let him inside, where he could see how poorly we lived. So we said our good-byes, and he was gone.

When I walked into our room, I found my parents huddled together on the floor. There was no news of Eunmi. My father was rocking back and forth, crying silently. He didn't dare make a noise because our neighbors would hear and know something was wrong. When they had asked him where Eunmi had gone, he said, "Oh, she's staying with friends." They could not know the truth or they would report us. So we waited that night, hoping Eunmi would return, but fearing something terrible had happened to her. All kinds of thoughts went through our heads. Not knowing was the hardest thing.

I was so tired and weak I went right to bed, and that's when I found a note from Eunmi under my pillow. It said, "Go find this lady. She will bring you to China." She gave me the address of a house near the river, across from the Wiyeon train station.

The next morning, my parents went to see the family of the girl who had run away with Eunmi. They brought the note with them. Then all of them went to the address Eunmi had left. When a woman came to the door, my mother demanded, "Where is our daughter? Tell me what you've done with her!"

The woman shook her head. "I don't know what you're talking about," she said. "I don't know your daughter."

There was nothing they could do, so they went home.

Days went by and there was still no word from Eunmi. On March 31, my father sent my mother on an errand to do some business. I was still very weak, but I was feeling well enough to walk a little bit, so I went with her. She was planning to stop by Eunmi's friend's house on the way, to see if they had heard any news about the girls.

When we arrived at the house, it was like a funeral was going on. Everybody was crying, and the girl's mother was frantic and sick with grief. "It's all my fault," she cried. She said her daughter was hungry all the time and was never satisfied with what her mother gave her to eat. "I told her she ate too much. But if I had known she was going to leave like this, I never would have said it." She couldn't stop sobbing, and her husband told her to please calm down. "You're going to die like this," he said. Quietly, he told my mother and me that it was better for his daughter to leave. She could not live in this country. And some of the other neighbor women were saying that they would go to China, too, if they had the chance.

After we left the house, my mother came up with another strategy. She was desperate to find out if Eunmi had crossed into China safely. She suggested that I return to the broker's house alone and tell

her that I wanted to go to China. We were hoping the broker would
let me in to look around, because for all we knew, my sister could still
be inside the house.

When I knocked on the door, the same woman answered. She was
in her early forties, like my mother, but she had a baby in her arms
who was still nursing. She was dressed very poorly, and when I peeked
inside the door, the house looked so run-down it seemed like it might
collapse at any moment. When she saw I was alone, she suddenly became very friendly. I told her I wanted to go to China, and she said
that could be arranged. Then I called my mother over. The woman
blocked the doorway and wouldn't invite us in, so we stood outside as
we spoke. At this point she didn't admit that she knew my sister, but
she seemed more eager to win our trust.

"Just wait here," she said.

She walked around the corner, then came back a little later and
led us to an alley. There she introduced us to a pregnant woman who
was also quite friendly.

"If you want, you can cross the river tonight," the pregnant woman
said.

I didn't know until that very moment how much I wanted to leave
North Korea. Even when I first knocked on the door I didn't know.
But right then and there I made up my mind. I was going to China,
and my mother was coming with me. Right now. It was not our original plan. My sister and I were supposed to go ahead, without my
mother. But now I knew I could not leave my mother behind.

I grabbed my mother's hands and said, "We must go, *Umma*! There
may never be another chance!" But my mother tried to pull away.

"Yeonmi-ya, I can't leave your father. He's sick. You have to go by
yourself."

I held on to her and said, "No, if I let go of your hands, you're going
to die in North Korea. I can't go if I leave you here!"

She begged me, "Just give me one chance to tell your father that I'm going. Then I'll come back."

I wouldn't let her leave, not even to tell my father. He would find a way to stop her, or she would change her mind. I knew if I let her out of my sight I would never see her again. So I said everything I could to persuade her to go with me now. I told her that we would find Eunmi and could settle in China first, and then we would get Father to come later. I still imagined we could come back any time to wave to my father across the river, just like those Chinese kids who used to ask me if I was hungry. But the most important thing, the only thing that really mattered, was that by tomorrow we wouldn't have to worry about food anymore. I gave her no choice.

I was still holding my mother's hands when I said to the pregnant woman, "I'll go if my mother can come, too."

"You can both go," she said.

"What about my sister, Eunmi?" I asked. "Will we find her there?"

"I'm sure of it," said the woman. "Once you cross the river, all the North Korean people live in the same area so you'll see her there."

This made sense to us, because it's the way North Korea would be organized, with different people assigned to different areas. We never thought to ask why these women were helping us, and why we didn't have to pay them anything. We didn't think that something might be wrong. Even though my mother worked in the black market, she trusted people. As North Koreans, we were innocent in a way that I cannot fully explain.

For the rest of the day we kept changing our location, with the pregnant woman making us wait outside different buildings on the outskirts of Hyesan. Finally, in late afternoon, we ducked into a public toilet and were given some very dark, thin clothes and ordered to change. The woman told us these clothes would make us look like the porters who smuggle goods across the river. That would be our story if we got caught. We would just say that we were being paid to pick up packages in China, and we planned to come right back.

Then she disappeared and two young men came out of the house. They led me and my mother down side streets and back alleys on our way out of town. They told us that if we traveled along the road, people would see us and there could be big trouble. So they took us on footpaths through the mountains—what we called those steep foothills where we went to gather wood—on a winding route back to the river. This was less than two weeks after my surgery and I was already exhausted. The boys walked really fast, and after a while I couldn't bear the pain in my side so I slowed them down a little. At first just the two boys led us along the trails, then another one joined us. He was even younger than the other boys, but he acted like he was the boss. He gave us more instructions about what we should do when we got to China.

"When you cross the river, don't tell anybody your real age," he said. "We've told the people on the other side that you are eighteen and twenty-eight years old. They won't take you if you're too young or too old. And don't let them know you are mother and daughter. They don't expect that and it will be a problem, too."

This seemed strange to me, but I had to trust these smugglers to know what was best to get us into China. By that time, we had walked all day, and it was getting dark. We hadn't had any food since the morning, and they gave us nothing to eat. At some point the first two stopped and told us to follow the youngest one. He led us to the edge of a cliff. It was very dark, but we could see a big road below us, and a steep bank down to the frozen river.

"Follow me," the boy said. "And whatever you do, don't make any noise."

PART TWO

China

Twelve

The Other
Side of Darkness

There was no time to rest on the other side of the river. We had made it past the North Korean soldiers, but Chinese patrols could still pick us up at any time and send us back across the border. Our guide told us to keep moving, so my mother and I followed him up the icy bank to a small unlit shack. A bald, heavyset man was waiting for us there.

"Here, give me your clothes and put these on," he said. We could tell by his rough accent that he must be one of the many Chinese of Korean descent who lived in Chaingbai. In the dark, we took off our clothes and put on another set of cheap Chinese clothes. Now if we were stopped, we might at least look like we belonged there. Our North Korean guide stayed with me while the bald broker pulled my mother around to the side of the building.

"Don't worry," the guide told me. "Everything is okay."

But it did not sound okay. I heard my mother pleading with this man, and then there were terrible noises I had never heard before.

It wasn't until later that I found out what happened. The broker told my mother that he wanted to have sex with me. She had to think quickly—he couldn't know I was her daughter and only thirteen. He might send us back to be captured by those border guards. So she explained to him I was too sick, that I had just had an operation and my stitches would tear.

"I'll be gentle," he said.

"No, you cannot!" my mother cried.

"What's it to you?" he said. "Why do you care about this girl?"

"I'm her aunt," my mother said. "We weren't supposed to tell you."

"What's going on here?" he said. "If you're going to be trouble, we'll just send you back to North Korea and they'll arrest you."

"We won't cause you any trouble," she said. "Take me instead."

He pushed my mother down on a blanket in the dirt, one he had obviously used before, and raped her.

A few minutes later, the broker reappeared around the building with my mother. Just then a car pulled up to the shack. All of us climbed in with the driver, my mother and I in the backseat, and we rode for a while along the river. I could sense something was badly wrong, but I still had no idea what my mother had done to protect me.

"*Umma*, what happened?" I asked. I kept forgetting not to call her "mother."

"Nothing, don't worry," she said, but her voice was shaking.

I was not used to traveling in a car, and I soon began to feel sick to my stomach. My mother put my head in her lap and held my hands tightly. But when we rounded a bend in the river, she told me to look up. From the window we could see the dark buildings on the North Korean side of the river.

"Look, Yeonmi-ya. That may be the last you see of your hometown," my mother said.

My heart jumped a little as we passed our apartment building. I knew my father was in there, waiting for us to come home. I swear I could see a flicker of light at the window, like a signal from my father to me. But my mother said no, it was my imagination. There was never a light.

Our next stop was the broker's apartment in Chaingbai.

"What's happening here?" my mother asked the young North Korean guide.

"Just listen to these people and everything will be fine," he said.

The bald broker's wife was ethnic Korean like himself, and paralyzed from the waist down. Her mother lived with them and took care of her. The broker's home had electricity, and now that he could see our faces clearly, he flew into a rage. "These women aren't eighteen and twenty-eight," he bellowed at the guide. My mother tried to stick to our story, and she was able to convince the broker that she was actually thirty-four instead of her true age of forty-one. But when he looked at me, he could tell I was just a child. The broker made a phone call and started arguing with someone in Korean. I could tell it was about money.

The wife, who was sitting up in her bed watching everything, finally explained what was going on.

"If you want to stay in China, you have to be sold and get married," she told us.

We were stunned. What did she mean, "sold"? I could not imagine how one human could sell another. I thought people could sell only dogs, chickens, or other animals—not people. And what did she mean, "get married"? I could not believe what was happening.

When we hesitated, the broker's wife lost her patience with us.

"Decide now! Decide!" she demanded. "Get sold or go back. That's the only way it works."

Ever since I had grabbed my mother's hands and refused to let go, a change had happened between us. From now on, I would be making the decisions. My mother looked at me and asked, "What do you want to do?"

Without thinking I said, "I want to eat something." We hadn't had a bite of food all day, and everything else was so confusing and terrifying that my focus became very narrow.

"Yes, Yeonmi-ya," she said. "But do you want to go back to North Korea?"

I thought for a short time. If we were sold, I figured that at least we would all be in the same village, and we could plan our next move when we got there. We could find Eunmi, and we could have something to eat.

"I want to stay in China," I said.

"Good," the bald broker said.

"Do you know anything about my older daughter, Eunmi?" my mother asked. "She was supposed to go to China and we haven't heard from her."

The bald broker told us he had expected to receive two girls a few days ago, but they never showed up. He had even tried again the day before we arrived, but couldn't make the connection. As far as he knew, they were still in North Korea. But he assured us that the girls would be in China soon, and that we could all meet in the village where the other defectors were living.

"Okay," I said. "We agree."

He made another call, and soon a very fat Chinese man and a skinny woman with a North Korean accent arrived. They sat down with the bald broker and negotiated our price right in front of us. The fat man, Zhifang, was another mid-level broker along the chain of traffickers who would eventually sell us to our "husbands." We learned that a mother with a young daughter would normally be sold together for a much lower rate than two healthy young women who could be sold separately. So the North Korean traffickers had lied to the bald broker, and now he was lying to this Chinese middleman, hiding the fact that we were mother and daughter and trying to convince him that I was really sixteen years old to get a higher price.

Zhifang kept looking at me and saying, "Come on, tell me your real age!"

There was no way I could convince him I was older because I was so little. I admitted that I was really thirteen.

"I knew it!" Zhifang said.

Finally, they reached a deal. My mother, who had been sold by the North Koreans for 500 Chinese yuan, the equivalent of about $65 (the value in 2007), was being bought by Zhifang for the equivalent of $650. My original price was the equivalent of $260, and I was sold to Zhifang for 15,000 yuan, or just under $2,000. The price would go up each time we were sold along the chain.

I will never forget the burning humiliation of listening to these negotiations, of being turned into a piece of merchandise in the space of a few hours. It was a feeling beyond anger. It's still hard to fathom why we went along with all of this, except that we were caught between fear and hope. We were numb, and our purpose was reduced to our immediate needs: Get away from the dangerous border. Get away from this terrible bald broker and his frightening wife. Get something to eat and figure out the rest of it later.

Once our prices were settled, the North Korean guide, Zhifang, and the woman all left the apartment. Then, finally, my mother and I were given something to eat. I couldn't believe it when the mother-in-law set a whole bowl of rice and some spicy pickled cucumber in front of me. I had never seen cucumber in winter, and it was like a miracle to taste it now. Eating all that rice seemed impossible. In North Korea, I would have to share my food with others and always leave something in the bowl. At home, eating all your food is rude and shameful, because you know your host will eat what you have left. But here in

China, there was so much rice that you were allowed to eat a whole bowl by yourself. And there was more food in the garbage can in this apartment than I might see in a week in Hyesan. I was suddenly very happy with my decision.

At five o'clock in the morning, with heavy snow blowing in circles around the apartment building, a taxi arrived and parked around the corner. We went outside, and the bald broker told me to wait by the gate. Then he threw my mother to the ground and raped her right in front of me, like an animal. I saw such fear in her eyes, but there was nothing I could do except stand there and shiver, begging silently for it to end. That was my introduction to sex.

When he had finished, the bald broker led us to the taxi and pushed us into the backseat. Both of us were shocked and speechless. There was another North Korean woman, in her early thirties, already inside. She had just crossed the border, too. Zhifang's helper, whose name was Young Sun, sat in the front, next to the driver. Young Sun explained to us that we were all going to another place before we were sold. My mother and I huddled together and tried to be calm. I was carsick most of the way, and very little was said as we drove through the Chinese countryside. At the end of the day, we finally stopped on the outskirts of what seemed to be a large city. My mother couldn't speak or read Chinese, but she had studied a little English in college. She saw a sign in both Chinese and Western characters that said we were in Changchun, the capital of Jilin province.

Already the air seemed different in China. In North Korea we lived in a haze of dust and burning trash. But in China the world seemed cleaner and you could smell wonderful things cooking everywhere.

Young Sun lived with Zhifang, the fat broker, in a neighborhood of modest apartment buildings—all of which seemed very fancy to me. After she let us into their apartment, the first thing she asked was, "What do you want to eat?"

"Eggs!" I said. "I want to eat eggs!"

I hadn't had more than a few bites of egg since my father was arrested, and then only at New Year's. But Young Sun fried five whole eggs and gave them to me. While I sopped up the rich yolks with soft bread, my opinion of China improved even more.

Later, we learned Young Sun's story. She had been some kind of smuggler in North Korea, where she got into debt and went broke. Zhifang offered her a job if she would come to China and live with him. Now, instead of transporting the women he bought at the border, he sent her instead. That way she took all the risk. She was living with him like a wife, but they were not married. She had no rights and no identification papers, so she could be arrested at any time and sent back to North Korea.

Virtually all defectors in China live in constant fear. The men who manage to get across often hire themselves to farmers for slave wages. They don't dare complain because all the farmer has to do is notify the police and they will be arrested and repatriated. The Chinese government doesn't want a flood of immigrants, nor does it want to upset the leadership in Pyongyang. Not only is North Korea a trading partner, but it's a nuclear power perched right on its border, and an important buffer between China and the American presence in the South. Beijing refuses to grant refugee status to escapees from North Korea, instead labeling them illegal "economic migrants" and shipping them home. We didn't know any of this, of course, before we escaped. We thought we would be welcomed. And in some places we were—just not by the authorities.

North Korean women were in demand in the rural areas of China because there were not enough Chinese women to go around. The government's population control strategy prohibited most couples from having more than one child—and in Chinese culture, a male child is more valued. Tragically, many female babies were aborted or, according to human rights groups, secretly killed at birth. China ended up with too many boys, and not enough women to marry them when they grew up. The ratio of male to female was especially unbalanced in the rural areas, where many local young women were lured to the big cities for jobs and a better life.

Men with physical or mental disabilities were particularly unlikely to find wives, and these men and their families created the market for North Korean slave-brides. But brides weren't cheap, sometimes costing thousands of dollars, or the equivalent of a year's earnings for a poor farmer. Of course, trafficking and slave marriages are illegal in China, and any children that result are not considered Chinese citizens. That means they cannot legally go to school, and without proper identification papers, can't find work when they get older. Everything about trafficking is inhuman, but it's still a big business in northeastern China.

After my mother and I and the other North Korean woman had eaten and rested, Zhifang, who had returned from Chaingbai separately, sat down with us to discuss what was going to happen next. He said another Chinese man would be coming by to take us to the countryside to match us with husbands.

"Can't we be sold together?" my mother asked. "This girl is really my daughter, not my niece."

The fat broker didn't seem surprised to hear this. "I'm sorry, but you and your daughter will have to be sold separately," he said. "I paid a price for each of you, and that's the only way I can get my money back."

"But my daughter can't get married," my mother said. "She's only thirteen."

"Look, don't worry. I agree she's too young," Zhifang said. "I'm a human being just like you! How could I sell a thirteen-year-old girl into marriage?" He told us that if my mother agreed to be sold separately, he and Young Sun would keep me with them, and raise me until I was older. Then they would make a decision. Meanwhile, they would give my mother their contact number so she could always be in touch with me.

My mother and I discussed it for a few minutes, and we agreed this was probably the best situation we could hope for.

My mother said yes, she would be sold without me.

"Good," Zhifang said. "Now, what else do you want to eat? If you want a watermelon, I will buy one for you tomorrow."

The next morning, Zhifang and Young Sun took me outside for my first real look at China. We walked by some shops, and I saw a mannequin for the first time in my life. I didn't know if it was a real person or a fake.

Young Sun saw me staring and said, "That's just a doll, little one."

I couldn't believe there were so many products in the stores. And there were restaurants and vendors selling all kinds of food. You could buy roasted corn on the street, and kebabs made out of kinds of fruit I had never seen before. The only one I recognized was a strawberry, which I had seen in a schoolbook.

"I want that one!" I said, pointing at the fruit.

They bought it for me, and I had my first taste of strawberry. I couldn't believe anything could taste so good. I could go on eating it forever. At first I was concerned that these luxuries were too expensive, but my new friends told me not to worry about it.

By now I thought that China had to be the best place in the world.

I had nearly forgotten the horrors of the past couple of days. My mind was filled with all the things I had to learn. I didn't like not understanding what people were saying around me, so I asked Young Sun to teach me a few words of Mandarin Chinese. The first were: *"Zhe shi shen me,"* which means "What is this?" Everywhere I went, I pointed and asked *"Zhe shi shen me?"* and Young Sun would give me the word.

During that first walk, Young Sun had to explain traffic patterns to me to keep me from walking into the road. We didn't have traffic lights in Hyesan, and there were very few cars anyway. In Pyongyang, I was too young to notice how it was done. But here you had to look up and watch for a signal before crossing or you would get run over. Before long it all became too overwhelming. I got dizzy seeing so many bright, different colors and people. The smell of gasoline and barbecue and car exhaust made me so sick I almost threw up in the street.

The couple steered me back toward the apartment. When we arrived, they told me it was time to say good-bye to my mother. Zhifang was going to take her and the other woman to the next man to sell them. Suddenly I snapped out of my dream. My mother was leaving and I was going to be left with strangers. She tried to be brave for me, and I could see the resolve in her delicate, weary face.

"Be a good girl," she told me. "Clean the house every day and cook for these people so they can see the value of keeping you here." She showed me the fat broker's phone number on a piece of paper folded in her pocket. "I'll call you as soon as I can. Maybe Eunmi will be waiting when I get there."

The night before, the brokers had given us soft Chinese white bread wrapped in plastic. It was so delicious that I decided to save half of mine to give to my mother to eat on her journey. But when I went to find it, the other North Korean woman had stolen it and eaten it herself. I had nothing to give my mother as we hugged good-bye.

. . .

I cried for a while after my mother was gone, so to cheer me up Zhifang and Young Sun took me out to a restaurant for dinner. It was the first time I had been to one since my trip to Pyongyang with my father. I had never seen disposable chopsticks before, and Zhifang and Young Sun showed me how to separate them without breaking them. Then they ordered huge plates of pork and peppers and fried rice. I ate until my stomach refused to take any more.

That night, Young Sun started teaching me some lessons in hygiene. I had never seen a toilet before, and she explained to me how to use it. I thought you were supposed to perch on top of it, like the drop toilets we used in North Korea. She showed me how to wash my hands in a sink, and reminded me of the proper way to use a toothbrush and toothpaste. We had been so poor after my father was arrested that we used salt on our fingers to brush our teeth. She also told me how Chinese women used disposable pads during their menstrual periods. Back in North Korea, we just used a thin cloth that we had to wash, so I had been confined to the house for days every month. When she handed me the soft cottony pad wrapped in thin plastic, I had no idea what to do with it. And it smelled so nice I wanted to save it for some other purpose. But I thought the concept was great because it gave women much more freedom.

The next day, she took me to a public bathhouse where women take showers together in one room. I had seen showers in movies, but this was my first experience. It was so wonderful to feel warm water coming down all over me. Young Sun scrubbed me from head to toe with real soap, and then she sprayed my head with something to kill the lice and put my hair in a shower cap. Everybody in North Korea had lice, and there was no way to get rid of them. So this treatment was a huge relief.

A few hours later, we were finished with my transformation. I had clean hair and new clothes when I walked back to the apartment. When Zhifang saw me, he smiled and said, "You look so shiny!"

Meanwhile, my mother and the North Korean woman who stole our bread had been sold to a *da laoban*, a "big boss" in the trafficking world who went by the name of Hongwei. There was a hierarchy of gangsters who specialized in North Korean bride trafficking, starting with the suppliers on the North Korean side of the border, through wholesalers like the bald Korean-Chinese broker in Chaingbai, and the couple in Chanchung. Kingpins like Hongwei were at the top of the chain, and often had a network of other retail brokers working for them.

Hongwei was Han Chinese—the majority ethnic group in China—and he didn't speak a word of Korean. He was tall and in his early thirties, with a long face and a full head of hair. As the group traveled by bus and taxi deep into China, my mother had no idea where they were going. They stopped for the night at a dark, cold house in the country. An old man arrived and built a fire for them, and Hongwei gestured to my mother that this was her husband; she had to sleep with him. But they had tricked her: it was just another broker. This ring of human traffickers always used the women before they were sold, including Hongwei. My mother had no choice but to accept it.

The next day, Hongwei took my mother and the other North Korean woman to a house in the country outside the city of Jinzhou, about three hundred miles northeast of Beijing. There he cleaned them up and gave them some new clothes and cosmetics. The other woman was sold quickly, but my mother took much longer to find a suitable match. For the next several days, Hongwei took her around to meet different men. She felt like a sack of potatoes in the market as they haggled over her price. The men said she was too skinny, or too old, and her price kept coming down. One woman brought her mentally damaged son to buy her, but my mother refused. (The brokers generally won't force women to accept matches, because they know they will just try to run away, which is bad for business. But if they are unreasonable, they will beat them or turn them over to the police to be sent back to North Korea.) Finally, a family of farmers arrived with a son who was in his early thirties and still unmarried. My mother was sold to them for the equivalent of about $2,100.

That day, they brought her to live in their farmhouse in what seemed like the middle of nowhere. It was very humble, built of stone and plaster with a metal roof. It was early April, so the fields were furrowed and ready to be planted with corn and beans. My mother had only a few words of Chinese by now, but she was able to show her new "husband" that she wanted to use his phone to call me. At first he refused, but after a few days of her crying and begging, he agreed. I was so happy to hear her when she called the fat broker's cell phone and he turned it over to me.

"Have you seen Eunmi?" I asked.

"No, little daughter," she said. "I haven't seen anybody else from North Korea."

I could tell by her voice that she was in terrible shape. She hadn't slept for days and she couldn't figure out how to tell her new family that she needed some sleeping pills, the kind she took at home when she could afford them. Now she was sorry that she had agreed to leave me behind. She couldn't protect me anymore, and she hadn't found my sister. I tried to make her feel better, telling her not to worry because everything was fine, and she had a phone number where she could reach me any time.

That was the last time she was able to make a call for many weeks.

The family locked up their cell phone, their money, even their food. She discovered that she was expected to be not just a wife to this Chinese farmer but a slave to his whole family. She had to cook and clean and work in the fields. Time after time she begged them to let her call her little daughter again, but no matter how much she cried, they didn't care. To them, she was like one of their farm animals, not a human being at all.

Thirteen

A Deal with the Devil

My mother had been gone for only three days when Zhifang tried to rape me.

His apartment was laid out with two bedrooms separated by a hallway. I was sleeping by myself across the hall from Zhifang and Young Sun when he crawled into my bed in the dark. He smelled of alcohol and his hands were rough when he grabbed me. I was so shocked that I started kicking him and struggling out of his grip.

"Quiet!" he whispered. "You'll wake her up!"

"If you don't let me go I'll scream!" I said. So he reluctantly left me alone and went back to his sleeping girlfriend.

A couple of days later, he tried it again. This time he gave Young Sun a lot of alcohol until she was passed out drunk, and then he came to my bedroom in the middle of the night. Again I fought him off by kicking and screaming and biting. I thought the only way to save myself was to act like a crazy person. I was so wild that he knew he would have to damage me badly or even kill me to finish what he started. And then I would have no value. So he gave up.

"Fine," he said. "But you can't stay in this house anymore. I'll sell you to a farmer."

"All right," I said. "Then sell me."

A few days later, the man who had bought and sold my mother returned to take me away.

Hongwei was not his real name, but then he lied about everything. He told me he was twenty-six, but he was actually thirty-two years old. He didn't know my real age because the fat broker Zhifang had told him I was sixteen. Nobody told the truth.

I was trying to learn Chinese, but I could understand very little. And Hongwei could communicate with me only in gestures. He took me to a Chinese restaurant for breakfast before our long journey. But I was so terrified that my hands were shaking. Every broker I had met in China had wanted to rape me, and I assumed this one was no different. Hongwei kept gesturing for me to eat, but I couldn't. Even though I was still skinny and malnourished, I no longer had an appetite. Food was the reason I had come to China, and now the thought of it made me sick.

We took a series of buses to Hongwei's home territory, which stretched from the ancient city of Chaoyang to the bustling port of Jinzhou. The buses made frequent stops, and at one of them a vendor came on board to sell ice cream to the passengers. Hongwei bought one for me. I hadn't eaten for a long time, and suddenly my appetite returned. I couldn't believe how something could be that delicious. I ate the whole thing and even kept eating it in my mind when it was finished.

That night we stayed at an inn in a small town outside Jinzhou. By the time we arrived that evening, I was again too upset to eat anything. So Hongwei took me to a grocery store to buy some supplies. I could tell he wanted me to pick out things that I needed, but I had never seen such luxury items, so I tried to tell him I didn't need anything. He went ahead and selected things for me. He picked out a fancy toothbrush, soap, and a pretty towel with embroidery. He saw that my skin was rough because of malnutrition and the cold, dry wind that blew in North Korea during the winters, so he bought me some moisturizing lotion. These things were so nice that I started to relax. I thought maybe he wasn't so bad after all.

When we arrived at the inn, he showed me a kind of cell phone that I had never seen before. Not only could you talk with it, but it played music and had a camera that took pictures. Hongwei was showing me how it could play back videos when my mother suddenly popped up on the screen, waving and saying hello. I got so excited I couldn't believe it.

"Umma! Umma!" I cried into the phone, grabbing it from his hands. I thought she was talking to me, so I tried to answer her. Hongwei was shocked. He had no idea that the woman he had just sold was my mother. Just like with me, he had been showing her the phone and took a video of her to demonstrate how it worked.

When I realized that my mother was not talking to me through the phone, my heart sank. But it was so good to see her face, and I thought this meant I would be seeing her in person soon.

Later that night, Hongwei gestured to me that he was my husband so I must sleep with him. Then he tried to rape me.

Again I fought back, kicking and biting and screaming like a madwoman. I made so much noise that I'm sure it sounded like a murder was taking place in our room. So Hongwei gave up and went to sleep. I spent the night with my back to the wall, staring out with bloodred eyes, waiting for him to try again.

The next morning, Hongwei tried to win me over with gifts and kindness. He took me to a store and bought me a pair of jeans, a sweater, and some running shoes. I had seen those kinds of shoes while I was secretly watching Chinese television in North Korea. It had been my dream to own a pair. Now that dream had come true and I was still miserable. I was beginning to realize that all the food in the world, and all the running shoes, could not make me happy. The material things were worthless. I had lost my family. I wasn't loved, I wasn't free, and I wasn't safe. I was alive, but everything that made life worth living was gone.

After a day in that small country town, Hongwei hired a taxi to take us into Jinzhou. He had rented a one-bedroom apartment in a four-story building in an older neighborhood near the zoo and a big park. To me it seemed like a nice place to live, but I was terrified to be there with Hongwei. Once again, he tried to rape me. Once again, I fought him off like someone with nothing to lose, like there was a demon inside me. I was so filled with fear and rage that even if he accidentally touched me in my sleep, I would start screaming and crying so hard that I couldn't stop. I would almost pass out, and I think it really scared him. Hongwei realized that he couldn't take me by force unless he was willing to destroy me.

So Hongwei locked me in a room in the apartment for days or weeks—I have no idea how long. He opened the door only to bring me food. But I still wouldn't change my mind. So one day he decided to try showing me the reality of my situation.

We traveled for two or three hours to a house in the countryside where Hongwei introduced me to a young, pregnant North Korean girl who lived with a Chinese man. Hongwei had her translate, just to make sure I understood him: if I refused to sleep with him, he was going to sell me off to a farmer. He wanted me to understand that he was offering me a much better alternative.

"Let him sell me," I said to the girl.

Hongwei shook his head in disbelief. He left me alone with her to think it over. She told me Hongwei was expecting to get a high price for me because I was a virgin and obviously very young.

I thought I could trust this girl because we were both North Koreans, and she would take pity on me. "Will you rescue me?" I asked her. "Can you help me escape and find my mother?"

She told her husband, and they agreed. We made a plan. While Hongwei was not paying attention, I slipped out the back door, jumped over a fence, and ran to a tumbledown old house in the woods. The girl's Chinese mother-in-law soon joined me. A few hours later, a man on a motorcycle arrived to take me to a house deep in the mountains that belonged to one of their relatives.

When I got there, I realized I had been tricked. The North Korean girl and her husband had stolen me from Hongwei, and now they were trying to sell me themselves. They came to visit me in the mountains with another broker, and the girl told me, "If you agree to sleep with this man, he will find you a rich young husband in a big city. You won't have to marry a farmer."

I still refused. I told them I would die before I let that happen.

The North Korean girl spent a week or so visiting with me while she tried to persuade me to be sold. I had a lot of time to practice my Chinese during this time, and I picked it up quickly.

Meanwhile, Hongwei had called in some of his gangster friends to help find me. They rode their motorcycles all over the area, searching houses and sheds for my hiding place. The couple who stole me told Hongwei that I had run away, but he didn't believe them. He tried threatening them to get me back, but they stuck to their story. The Chinese man who had taken me even offered to help in the search.

Through his connections in the trafficking world, Hongwei eventually learned where I was being hidden. He approached the couple with a deal: Unless they cooperated with him, he would report them to the police, and the girl would be sent back to North Korea. But if they returned me unharmed, he would pay to buy me back. They took the deal. So Hongwei bought me twice. I never learned the exact figure, but I know it was a lot more than the price he had paid to buy me from Zhifang.

When another man on a motorcycle showed up at my mountain hiding place, I thought that I was finally being rescued. Instead he took me into town, where Hongwei was waiting with a group of hard-looking men.

"Are you all right?" Hongwei asked. "Did they hurt you?"

I shook my head no. I could understand more of what he said now, but I didn't want to speak to him.

Usually when North Korean slave-brides run away from their brokers, they are badly beaten or even killed. But Hongwei didn't do that. He seemed so happy to have me back that he bought a big restaurant dinner for all the gangsters who had helped him in the search. We took a bus back to Jinzhou that night.

As we walked from the bus station to the apartment, I was feeling very strong and calm, because I had already made the decision to kill myself instead of accepting this life. I had lost control of everything else, but this was one last choice I could make. I had cried every single day since I left North Korea, so much that I couldn't believe I had that many tears inside of me. But on the last day of my life, there would be no more crying.

Just as I had given up, Hongwei was filled with hope. He was not a religious man, but he sometimes prayed to the Buddha. The whole concept of religion was foreign to me. In North Korea, we worshipped only the Kim dictators, and our faith was in *juche*, the doctrine of nationalistic self-determination created by Kim Il Sung. Practicing any other religion is strictly forbidden and could get you killed. But in North Korea, fortune-tellers are popular (although not officially sanctioned), and many people are superstitious about dates and numbers. So I understood Hongwei's extremely superstitious nature. He counted the steps as he walked to the apartment, and when we got there, he burned the same number of joss papers—fake money that is sent to the afterworld as offerings to ancestors. He hoped this would bring him luck with me. But it did not work.

Once again he tried to rape me. He pinned my arms to the bed, but I bit him and kicked him hard and got away. I ran to the kitchen and grabbed a knife, then held it to my throat as I stood on the balcony.

I was raving and screaming in Korean, "If you come near me, I'll jump!" He couldn't understand what I was saying, but he could see in my eyes that I was ready to die.

Hongwei spoke in a soothing voice, saying *"Biedong, biedong,"* which means "Don't move" in Chinese. He used simple words that I could understand, and gestures to describe a bargain he had in mind. "You be my wife," he said. "Mama come. Papa come. Sister come."

Suddenly, he had my attention. I slowly put down the knife. We sat down and, still using pantomime and simple words, he laid out his offer: If I would live with him as his *xiao-xifu*, or "little wife"—meaning mistress—he would find my mother and buy her back. Then he would find my father in North Korea and pay for a broker to bring him to China. And he would help me find my sister.

And if I didn't do this? He obviously couldn't sell me, so he would turn me in to the Chinese police. I would never let this happen, of course.

I couldn't really think logically at the time, but I recognized an opportunity to do something that was not just for me. I had thought only of myself for most of my life. But now I had a chance to choose my family over my own pride. I was willing to die to avoid the shame of being raped. But now I had another choice: to die selfishly or to save my family.

But first I had to consider: could I trust this man?

Everything I had been told since I left North Korea had been a lie. But something about the way Hongwei presented this bargain made me believe he was sincere. After all, he had been so determined to find me after I ran away. He knew that if he didn't keep his word, I would kill myself, and in his own barbaric way he seemed to have genuine feelings toward me.

In the end there was no choice at all.

For a long time I thought of it as a business negotiation, not rape. Only now, with the passage of time, can I accept what transpired in all its terrible dimensions. I was only six months past my thirteenth birthday, and small for my age. When Hongwei pressed himself on top of me, I thought I would split in two. I was so scared, and the act was so painful and disgusting and violent that I thought it couldn't really be happening to me. After a while I actually felt like I had left my body and was sitting on the floor next to the bed. I was watching myself, but it wasn't me.

As soon as Hongwei was finished with me, I went to the bathroom and showered for what seemed like hours. I felt so dirty. I felt such despair. I rubbed my skin until I bled, and that made me feel a little better. I discovered that physical pain helped me feel less pain inside, and for a while pinching and scratching myself with a rough cloth became a habit. Sometimes it was the only way to escape the aching in my heart.

Yeonmi's parents at a zoo in Pyongyang,
the capital of North Korea

ABOVE: Yeonmi on
her first birthday

RIGHT: Yeonmi at one
hundred days old

Yeonmi around age two

Yeonmi (right), her paternal grandfather (middle), and her older sister, Eunmi (left)

ABOVE: Yeonmi and Eunmi sledding, around ages three and five, respectively

LEFT: Yeonmi dressed for the snow, three years old

Yeonmi and Eunmi, prepared
for a snowy day

1996.9.9 기념

Yeonmi, age three (right),
and Eunmi, age five (left)

LEFT: Family photo, 1996. Yeonmi is three and Eunmi is five.

BELOW: Yeonmi and her family in Hyesan, a North Korean city on the border with China

Yeonmi at three years old

Yeonmi and Eunmi dressed for the snow

ABOVE: Family photo in Hyesan

LEFT: Yeonmi and Eunmi in matching outfits

Yeonmi (third row, second from left)
and Eunmi (second row, left) at a family
wedding in the countryside

Yeonmi around eight years old
in Pyongyang

ABOVE: Yeonmi's father in
Pyongyang before his arrest

LEFT: Yeonmi and her father
before his arrest

The final photo Yeonmi and her mother
took of her father before his death

Together again: Eunmi, mother, and Yeonmi, Seoul 2015

When Hongwei checked to see why the shower was running so long, he found me on the bathroom floor, limp and nearly drowned. He didn't say a word as he carried me back to bed, but I could see that tears were running down his face.

I felt like I was losing my mind. The sexual act was so repulsive that I threw up every night. For a long time I couldn't eat more than a few spoonfuls of rice in a day. Eventually I became numb, and Hongwei thought I was recovering. But I was just going through the motions of being alive while watching myself from a distance, like I was playing a role in a movie that never seemed to end. All that was left inside me was a smoldering hatred for this man. I fantasized about killing him in his sleep and running away. But where would I go now? And who else could save my family?

"We'll find your mother soon," Hongwei told me one morning. "But there's more to this deal. You will need to help me with my business."

I had been in China for just two months when I began working for Hongwei. He brought two North Korean girls to stay in the apartment, and I talked to them and was able to translate a little. I cleaned them up, just as Young Sun had done for me, picked out clothes and makeup for them, and gave them lessons in hygiene. Unlike my mother and me, these girls had known they would be sold in China when they escaped. They didn't care, they said. It was better than dying in North Korea.

Hongwei brought me with him to help sell these women in the countryside. After that business was finished, we returned to the village where he had sold my mother, and I met with her Chinese "husband." I spoke enough Chinese by now that I was able to tell him I wanted to buy my mother back. We negotiated a price—it was my first real business transaction. Hongwei paid a little more than $2,000 to buy her back for me, and I was secretly pleased he lost money on the deal.

A few days later, we met the family in a secret location in the countryside to make the exchange. It was June, and the grass was high. My mother saw me from far away and came running down a dirt lane to hug me. She had no idea what had happened to me, or that I was coming to get her. One time she had managed to sneak a call to the fat broker Zhifang in Changchun, but all he would tell her was that I was gone. We were so happy to see each other we couldn't stop crying from joy. It was the first time I had smiled or even felt alive in many weeks.

Out of habit, my mother pulled me up on her back for a piggyback ride, just like when I was a baby.

"Let me see how much my little puppy grew while I was gone," she said. But I was not a little puppy anymore. She later told me she had hardly recognized me in my makeup and new clothes. I didn't recognize me either. I no longer looked like a child, and everything that was childlike inside me was gone. It was as if the blood had dried in my veins and I'd become another person. I didn't have pity for anyone, including the girls I helped sell, including myself. My only purpose now was to bring my family together again.

There was no word of my sister. Hongwei told us that he had asked the other brokers if they knew what happened to her, but he learned nothing. It was a disappointment, but I still had hope that he could use his network to find her. And soon we would be seeing my father again.

My mother left that terrible farm without looking back. The three of us returned to Jinzhou together.

I still hated Hongwei, but I learned to live with him. He was sometimes very harsh with me in the beginning, but he softened with time, and I think he grew to respect me, trust me, and, in his own way, love me.

His life had never been easy. Hongwei was born on a farm west of Chaoyang, an ancient city of Buddhist temples, parks, skyscrapers, and street gangs. When he was twelve or thirteen, he ran away to the city and joined a gang that controlled a string of karaoke clubs. These weren't the kind of friendly sing-along bars you might find in Seoul or other cities. They were places where women provided more entertainment than just serving drinks. Hongwei never had a higher education, but he could read and write and was very smart. By fifteen, he was the head of his gang with his own karaoke empire. He used his connections to get into a lot of different businesses, such as restaurants and real estate development. About two years before I escaped from North Korea, he branched out into human trafficking. For a while, that's where the big money was.

In Chaoyang, Hongwei had a Chinese wife and two children, a son and a daughter. The daughter, I later learned, was only a year younger than I was.

After Hongwei bought back my mother, she told him my true age was thirteen, not sixteen. I had never bothered telling him my age because I couldn't believe it would matter. But he seemed shocked.

"I would never have slept with her if I'd known she was so young," he said.

I don't know if that was true, but after that he began treating me a little more gently, and I almost started seeing him as a human being. But I still expected him to live up to all of his promises, including rescuing my father from North Korea. Hongwei had contacts in Chaingbai, including some women whose business was to run errands back and forth across the border. They were hired to transfer money to North Koreans whose relatives on the outside wanted to help them. They also smuggled in Chinese cell phones so families that were separated could stay in contact. This was very dangerous, but it could be arranged for the right price.

In August, Hongwei hired one of these brokers to find my father.

Fourteen

A Birthday Gift

August 15 is a big holiday in North Korea because it celebrates the day in 1945 that Japan surrendered. On that day in 2007, our agent finally located my father in our old apartment outside Hyesan. He had no phone of his own, and it would have put him in danger to try to contact him any other way. So the woman we'd hired handed him a Chinese cell phone. He was crouching on the balcony, looking out at the Yalu River, when I called at the appointed time.

"*Abuji?* It's Yeonmi! *Umma* and I are okay. How are you?"

There was quiet on the other end. He couldn't believe he was hearing my voice after nearly five long months.

"I'm doing fine, little daughter," he said finally. "I'm so happy to hear your voice. Where are you?" We didn't have much time to talk, because the police are always scanning for illegal calls. I was able to tell him only that we were in China and my mother and I were safe. We hadn't found Eunmi yet, but we were still looking for her.

"I miss you so much, Father," I said. "I'll bring you to China. We'll pay a broker to bring you to us."

"Please don't worry about me," he said.

"Just come, Father," I said. "I'll take care of everything." I told him we could look for Eunmi together when he arrived.

"Okay," he said. "I'll come."

He cried all night after the agent left him.

My father had searched for us for a long time after we escaped. He went back to the address Eunmi had left for me and learned that the woman who trafficked us was named Jo Yong Ae. When he demanded that she tell him what happened to his wife and daughters, she admitted that she had sent me and my mother to China. But Yong Ae claimed she knew nothing about Eunmi. My father had no idea what had happened to us after we crossed the border. All Yong Ae would tell him was that we had gone to a place where there was food for us. He could only hope that we would contact him.

After we left, his brother and our former neighbor arranged for a woman to live with him and do his cooking and cleaning. They all thought my mother would never come back. He told us he couldn't sleep, couldn't eat, couldn't stop crying.

Meanwhile, many people who knew us thought that my father was the one who had sent us to China. After all, he was a clever man with many connections. How could he not know where we had gone?

The teenage girls who shared the apartment with us were convinced that my father could help them get to China, too. They were very poor and desperate. He told them he was unable to help them, but they continued to beg, telling him they couldn't live in North Korea anymore.

Finally, he agreed to help them escape on the condition that they tell their mother before they left. He gave them Yong Ae's address and the girls left through her, without telling their mother. They knew she would have never let them go. When she discovered that her daughters had left, she blamed my father. He later told my mother that Yong Ae had given him 100 yuan, about $13 worth of Chinese money, for sending her the girls. He said he felt bad about it because it had caused the girls' mother so much pain. But he never knew they were being sold as brides—or that that was what had happened to me and my mother. He just thought some rich Chinese people were paying to adopt North Koreans.

It took six more weeks to arrange a successful escape for my father. I knew he was still very sick, although I assumed he was just working too hard and not eating enough. When I spoke to my father again, I told him that I would feed him and make him healthy again in China.

"Yes, of course," he said. He was always so optimistic, and he never complained about his pain. But I could hear the weakness in his voice. There was no time to waste.

I had come to like our nice apartment and the Jinzhou neighborhood, where I could enjoy the nearby park and market. But we were soon on the move again.

There was a flower shop on the main street in front of our building, and it fascinated me because I had never seen one before. In North Korea, if you want flowers, you go out and pick some. But here there were whole stores filled with beautiful blooms. I would sometimes slip into the shop just to breathe in the sweet, spicy fragrance, even though I never bought anything. The lady who owned the shop started to recognize me. Soon she smiled and waved every time she saw me. It made me nervous because I knew if anyone discovered I was an illegal North Korean, the police would be after us. When I told Hongwei about my concerns, he packed up the apartment and we moved the next day. We would probably have left soon anyway, because it was too risky to stay in one place very long.

The next apartment was a large studio with a kitchen and bathroom in a different part of the city. Sometimes we'd have as many as nine women sleeping on the floor of that place, waiting to be sold.

While my mother stayed behind and took care of the apartment, Hongwei sent me out to do his business, just as Zhifang had used Young Sun. I would be the one taking all the risks, traveling all over the countryside with illegal refugees. I had to pretend I was much older, because the women wouldn't listen to a thirteen-year-old girl. My job was to translate for them, buy tickets or hire taxis to bring them back to Hongwei, and persuade them to cooperate if they wanted to stay in China. Once they met their potential husbands, I told the men that these women would learn Chinese as I had, and be faithful wives to them. I told the women that these men were gentle and rich, so they could send some money to their relatives.

I tried to make it go easier for the women I sold, but sometimes I could not. The brokers were rapists and gangsters, and many of the women suffered terribly. One young woman, about twenty-five years old, had jumped off a bridge onto a frozen river during her escape. By the time she arrived in Chanchung, she could no longer move the lower part of her body. She told me that Zhifang had raped her anyway. Hongwei still managed to sell her to a farmer. It was horrible. Sadly, there were many cases like hers, some even worse.

It makes me sick to think about what I and so many girls and women had to do to survive in China. I wish it had all never happened, and that I never had to talk about it again. But I want everyone to know the shocking truth about human trafficking. If the Chinese government would end its heartless policy of sending refugees back to North Korea, then the brokers would lose all their power to exploit and enslave these women. But of course if North Korea wasn't such a hell on earth, there wouldn't be a need for the women to flee in the first place.

M ost of the time Hongwei sold women as brides for Chinese men, but sometimes the women asked him to sell them into prostitution, where they could make money to send back to their families. When I arrived in China, I had no idea what a prostitute was. Then one day, Hongwei took me on a trip with him to a steamy seaport called Huludao, where a lot of South Korean men and other tourists came for cut-rate sex. He was dropping off a woman at a brothel and he needed me to translate.

The brothel in Huludao was run by a middle-aged Chinese woman, who went out of her way to be friendly to me. She showed me the nice desk in her office and gave me a tour of the hallways lined with tiny, curtained rooms just large enough for a small platform bed. There was a shower room, too, although I couldn't understand why people were using it in the middle of the day.

I met several North Korean women there, including a beautiful girl from Pyongyang who had been working in the brothel for seven years. All the women told me what a great place it was if I wanted to earn money, plus I could eat kimchi and other Korean food every day and meet all kinds of South Koreans. I was thrilled by this, because I wanted to meet a South Korean with a lovely accent, like the ones I had seen on videos. The girls made it all sound really great, and the madam offered me a place with her.

When I told Hongwei that I wanted to stay with the nice lady, he said, "Are you crazy? Don't ever think about working in a place like this!"

"No, I want you to sell me to her!" I said.

That's when he slapped me across the face.

"You don't understand anything I tell you!" he said.

He finished his business and got me out of there as fast as he could.

I made several trips back to Huludao in the coming months, and I learned what I would have gotten myself into if I had stayed. Customers paid about $5 to sleep with the women, and the women got to keep $1. That was actually an excellent percentage for a brothel, which was why the women wanted to work there. But you had to have sex with up to a dozen men a day, some of them farmers so filthy you couldn't wash the smell off of them. Yet there were places far worse than this.

Hongwei told me about hotels in Beijing and Shanghai where girls who wanted to leave were injected with drugs to turn them into addicts. Then they could never run away.

There is no doubt that trafficking is an ugly and brutal business. But whenever human beings are thrown together, no matter what the circumstances, we find ways to connect with one another. We can cry and laugh together, even in the worst times. My mother and I got to know the women who passed through our lives, and some became our friends.

Myung Ok was in her early forties, from Hyesan, and had escaped from North Korea twice. The first time, she made it across the river with a daughter who was around my age, and they were sold together. But while they were living with her Chinese husband, the police captured and repatriated them. The daughter was too young for a prison camp, so she was sent for "reeducation"—which meant she was starved and beaten for weeks. Myung Ok was sent to a labor camp, where she was tortured and worked almost to death.

After her release, Myung Ok decided to risk another escape, although her daughter was too afraid and stayed behind. Myung Ok made it across a second time and ended up being trafficked by Zhifang, who sold her to Hongwei. My mother and Myung Ok got along well because they both came from Hyesan and Myung Ok had a great sense of humor.

Unfortunately, Hongwei sold Myung Ok to a handicapped farmer who treated her badly. The man was so nervous about her running away that he followed her everywhere, even into the bathroom. She couldn't take it anymore and managed to escape to the bustling northeastern city of Shenyang, where there was a large population of North Korean defectors in hiding. But Hongwei had underworld connections in Shenyang, and his men found her and beat her up. She was sent back to the farmer again. If she had succeeded in running away, Hongwei would have had to refund the farmer's money; his women came with a limited one-year warranty, just like a car.

Until my mother and I heard the stories told by Myung Ok and other women we met, we never really understood the dangers of being caught by the police and sent back to North Korea. There were even worse stories about women carrying half-Chinese babies who were forced to abort them, or being executed if the North Koreans found them trying to defect to South Korea. After this, my mother and I made an oath that we would never be taken alive.

The first time my father tried to escape to China was in September 2007. I had told him someone would come to get him once he waded across the river. But when he reached the other side, nobody was waiting for him. Hongwei had paid the fat broker to arrange the escape, but he had failed. My poor father had to evade the soldiers again to make his way back to North Korea.

He tried again on October 1. By then, the river was running high and cold. This time Hongwei traveled to Chaingbai to make sure nothing went wrong. He paid the broker Zhifang the equivalent of $1,300 for my father—a very high price for a man escaping from North Korea. Hongwei was shocked when he met my father and saw how skinny and weak he was. He had hoped to put him to work so that he could pay off his debt. But now he realized my father was too sick even to travel by bus, so Hongwei hired a taxi to take him and two women he had bought all the way to Jinzhou.

They arrived on October 4, 2007, my fourteenth birthday, six months after I'd arrived in China. When my mother and I saw my father walk in the door, we ran into his arms. I could hardly believe I had both my parents with me again. And it was the first time in many years that my father had been around to celebrate my birthday. Usually he was traveling for his business, or later, he was in prison. So Hongwei decided to throw a very special celebration. While my parents and I were crying and hugging and talking, Hongwei went out and brought back all kinds of food and drinks for us. I had told him my father loved meat, so he bought duck, chicken, beef, and pork. There were a few North Korean women living with us in the apartment at the time, and Hongwei had brought some others along with my father, so we had a big party. The meal was like a dream come true for my father, but it was heartbreaking because he was too weak to eat any of it.

That night, he showed me and my mother a plastic bag of opium that he had brought to kill himself with if he was captured on the way across the border. He said he would also use it if he was arrested in China, because he would not be sent back, or risk revealing our location to the police. But he was very happy to have made it out alive to see his family again. All that was missing was Eunmi. We still had no news, but my father was full of hope. He had plans to search for her after he got treatment for his stomach. And then maybe he would find a way to start a business so that he could take care of us again. My uncle Min Sik was right when he told my mother that her future husband was like a plant that could grow out of solid rock.

My father quickly came to understand my arrangement with Hongwei. It broke his heart to see his young daughter exploited by this older man, but the reality was more complicated, and like my mother and me, he had mixed feelings about Hongwei. My father was grateful that Hongwei had kept his word and saved my mother, grateful that I hadn't been sold off to a farmer and lost forever. He knew things could have been so much worse for me. He thanked Hongwei for bringing him to China and allowing him to live under his roof. But underneath he hated Hongwei, too. My father could hardly recognize me now, with my made-up face and manicured nails. I was a different person, responsible for the lives of my parents and so many others. Yet there was nothing he could do about it and no way to take the burden from me. He had to rely on me for everything. And he was so sick.

My father was not the kind of man to reveal his deep feelings or show any weakness. He always smiled at me and told me everything would be great. I was so thankful that he treated me like an adult. But I could also tell he was crushed to see me robbed of my childhood. The only time he hinted at his feelings was once when he hugged me close and breathed in my scent. "You've lost your sweet baby smell, Yeonmi-ya," he said gently. "I miss the way you smelled as a child."

My mother and I wanted to hear all the news from Hyesan. My father told us about his brother's sons, who were hoping to become doctors, and his sisters in Pyongyang and Hyesan. His younger sister in Hyesan was a widow who had very bad luck in life. Both she and her daughter, who was about my age, suffered from tuberculosis.

My father asked me to look after them and the rest of the family if anything happened to him.

Chun Guen had gone into the military, as we all knew he would. Even after I disappeared, he was faithful to me. My father said he came by our apartment to look for me. "Where's Yeonmi?" he asked. He looked so sad and anxious. There was nothing my father could tell him.

M y father needed to check into a modern Chinese hospital as soon as possible for an examination and tests. But there was a problem: he was an illegal. We couldn't even pretend that he was a North Korean visiting relatives because his identification papers had been destroyed when he went to prison. And so admitting him to a proper hospital would be very expensive and risky. The staff might turn him in to the authorities. So instead we took him to a small clinic that would not ask too many questions. My father was still in terrible pain, and even though he was hungry, he was too nauseated to eat. The clinic doctor examined him and told us he thought his case was too serious for them to handle. "You have to get him to a hospital right away," she told us. But we couldn't do that. So she gave him some medicine that might help the pain. When we got him home, he was white, as if his blood had drained from his veins. We decided we had to risk our lives to get him admitted to a hospital.

Hongwei was not happy about this situation, but he agreed to help us register him. In early November, just a month after he arrived in China, my father was wheeled into the operating room of a hospital in Jinzhou. The surgeons opened his stomach and closed him right back up.

We could see the bad news on the face of the doctor who he came out to talk to us.

"I'm afraid there is nothing we can do," he said. "This patient has advanced colon cancer and it has spread to all his organs." He explained that there were so many tumors it was pointless trying to operate. My father might have three to six months to live, at the most. All we could do was try to keep him comfortable.

Fifteen

Dust and Bones

My mother did not understand, so I had to explain what the doctor told us. All I really understood was that my father was going to die very soon. I didn't know anything about cancer because it is so uncommon in North Korea. This wasn't to say the disease didn't exist; it probably just went undiagnosed. Most people didn't die of cancer because other things killed them first.

My mother and I couldn't bring ourselves to tell my father what the doctors had found. It was so pitiful; he woke up from his operation thinking everything would be all right.

We had to get him out of the hospital as soon as possible, so we brought him back to the apartment to recover. As soon as the anesthesia wore off, the pain came back. He couldn't eat anything. His condition grew worse every day, and we couldn't afford the kind of painkillers he needed, or the IV drip that would have made him more comfortable, or the nutritional supplements that might have extended his life. The operation had been so expensive that I was afraid to ask Hongwei for more money.

"Why am I not getting better, little daughter?" he kept asking me. "If they can't help me in China, maybe I should go back to North Korea." He also felt guilty about his family. We had found out that his brother and sisters had been questioned by the police after he escaped. My uncle Park Jin's sons were forced to leave the military and their careers as doctors were all in danger. My aunt in Hyesan had been tortured when she was interrogated. My father regretted his decision, and he wanted to go back to help them. He thought he could tell the police he never defected, that he just went to China for medical treatment.

That's when my mother and I had to tell him that he had cancer, and the doctors had given him no hope of survival.

"Then I will go back to die in the country where I was born," he said.

We had to beg him not to ask us to take him back. He was too sick to travel, and if he made it to Hyesan, he would die in prison. "*Abuji,* who will take care of you there?" I said sadly. "And who will bury you?"

After that, he stopped talking about going back to North Korea.

The next months were very hard. The Chinese government had started cracking down on human traffickers, and Hongwei's business had become more dangerous and less profitable. It was 2008 and the whole country was preparing for the Beijing Summer Olympics. Later I learned that Western governments and human rights groups had been pressuring China to improve its treatment of internal migrants, ethnic minorities, and political dissenters. According to news reports that we never heard, Beijing responded by rounding up anybody who might embarrass the government and ruin China's great international triumph. All we knew at the time was that the police were getting more expensive to bribe, and they were hunting down and repatriating North Korean refugees at a record pace. More and more, potential customers were afraid to pay for Hongwei's women because the police might raid their farms and take the women away.

Hongwei was increasingly angry and on edge. He spent most of his time in the countryside trying to sell the women he had already bought and he wanted me to be with him to help him. I was torn between spending time with my dying father and doing Hongwei's business for him.

My mother and I had no pictures of my father with us, and we felt it was very important to have one taken so that he could be remembered. He was too sick to go out, so we arranged for a photographer to come to the apartment to take some photos. My father wore a nice sweater we had bought for him in China. My mother and I were wearing our best clothes and full makeup. I was draped in gold that Hongwei had bought for me. We propped my father up in bed between me and my mother, and he managed a thin smile for the pictures. I looked ten years older than my true age. My father was so skinny that I can barely recognize him in those photographs. Our poses were forced and formal. Death occupied the spaces between us.

As my father grew worse, even breathing was painful for him, and he could not go to the bathroom by himself, which was a terrible fate for such a dignified man. Still, he never complained. As he was fading, all my father wanted was to be with me. But I was too young to understand what death meant. Even after he passed away, I thought I was going to see him again because he had always managed to come back to me.

When I was able to spend time with him, he often wanted to talk about when he was a child. I listened to him tell stories, describing how he had nearly electrocuted himself while he was playing with friends in Hyesan. He touched a live wire with both hands and was thrown through the air. He woke up in the hospital in a vat of water they were using to draw off the electricity. Mostly he spoke about his childhood with a warm nostalgia. When he was young, he said, the public distribution system was so great that he and his friends would get candy every month.

On his good days, we played Chinese checkers to pass the time. He was always the best player when we lived in North Korea, and I won only a few games with him in my life. But now I was able to beat him. I wasn't going to show mercy, even if he was sick! One day he smiled and pulled me close and kissed the top of my head, breathing deeply.

"Yeonmi-ya, it's you," he said. "I smell that baby smell again."

Hongwei grew increasingly aggravated that he had to take care of all three of us, and things were as tense as I could remember. One night Myung Ok, the woman Hongwei had recaptured after she escaped to Shenyang, got drunk in the apartment and was making too much noise. When Hongwei lunged to slap her, I tried to jump between them and he hit me instead. The household was falling into chaos. It got even worse after we returned Myung Ok to her Chinese farmer and she ran away again. Hongwei was forced to go back to his village to make good on his guarantee.

In early January, my mother called me while I was in the country-side with Hongwei.

"Yeonmi, you have to come now," she said. "Your father is going to die very soon."

I could hear the panic in her voice. I took a taxi back to Jinzhou and found my father in bed, incoherent.

"Is that you, Yeonmi?" he said. He held my hand but couldn't see me. "Is that you, my daughter? Where's my daughter?"

I don't know if he was calling out for me or for Eunmi, who had been lost for the past nine months. My mother told me that he found her sleeping pills and had taken all of them. He wanted to kill himself so that he wouldn't cause any more trouble for me.

"Oh, Father," I sobbed. "Please don't worry. Everything will be fine. I'll be here."

But of course it was not, and I could not stay. Hongwei kept calling, insisting that I come back and help him finish selling the women. But my father's spirit was so strong that it would not leave his body. Eventually I had to tell my mother that I had to go but would be back as soon as I could get away.

My father held on for weeks. I kept returning by bus or taxi to check on him, and it usually took me several hours of travel each way. Hongwei got angrier and more violent. One time he threw a heavy glass at me that hit me behind the ear. Another time he slapped me right in front of my father. I have no idea how I survived that terrible time.

Finally, my father couldn't speak anymore, and Hongwei brought me back for the last time to say good-bye. I kept hugging my father and asking him, "What do you need? What can I do?" But he couldn't answer. All he could do was open his eyes to tell me he had heard me. I held his hand and saw that his fingernails had grown so long. "This is something I can do," I told him. I carefully clipped the nails on one hand, rubbing his fingers gently as I worked. He fell asleep before I could do the other hand.

"We can finish this tomorrow," I said, then curled up on the floor next to him.

I woke up at 7:30 the next morning and saw that he had stopped breathing. His body was still warm, so I lay next to him and held him.

His eyes were open and I could not close them, no matter how long I held my fingers to his lids. In Korea we say that if a person cannot close his eyes in death, it is because he hasn't fulfilled something in this world. I think my father was still searching for Eunmi, and that was why he could not rest. I thought that I would be like my father and never close my eyes until I had found my sister.

I was crazy with grief and refused to leave my father's body. I just couldn't believe I would never see him again. I tried talking to him, thinking he might wake up. It was impossible to accept that the strongest man I had ever known could just die and there was nothing I could do. I finished clipping his nails and I brushed his hair. I washed his face with a towel and put a blanket around him to keep him warm. I stayed by his side until night fell and we had to move his body.

We had discussed my father's burial with him while he was still able to talk. He didn't want to be cremated because he hated the idea of burning up, but he knew he wanted to be buried in North Korea someday, and cremation was the only way that would be possible. When I was ready to let him go, my mother and I wrapped his body in a sheet of heavy paper, the kind used to protect floors during construction. At midnight, two men who worked for Hongwei helped us put him in the back of a car.

Hongwei decided it was time to move apartments again, so we packed our few belongings and headed north to Chaoyang. He knew a place where my father would be cremated secretly. Even in death we had to hide from the authorities. When we arrived, the men backed the car up to the crematorium and unloaded my father's body. My mother and I watched as they rolled him into the fire and shut the door. For the first time since my father died, I began to sob. Soon my mother was crying with me, but the men told us to be quiet, people might hear us.

It took an hour or so for the flames to finish their work. When it was over, there was nothing left but dust and bones. We had to leave quickly or risk being discovered, so I began to scoop my father's ashes into a box I'd brought with me. The man who worked the machine offered me gloves because the remains were still very hot, but I brushed them aside. I gathered the grit and bone chips in my bare hands to feel his weight; in the end, there was so little left of him.

We drove out of town for a couple of hours until we reached the small town of Yangshanzhen, where there was a house where we could stay. We had already decided to bury my father's ashes in a secret place nearby, on the top of a small mountain looking over a river. He always loved sunshine and water. My mother stayed behind at Hongwei's friend's house while Hongwei and his men led me through the fields and up the mountainside. I hugged my father as I followed them through the bitter cold night. The men dug a hole in the frozen ground. Then I put my father's picture inside the box, and I faced the box toward the flowing river, so that my father could see it while he waited for me to return.

I had never felt so alone in my life.

Sixteen

Kidnapped

Hongwei was running out of money. The Chinese government crackdown on human trafficking in the months before the 2008 Summer Olympics had destroyed his business, so he needed another way to earn income. We moved again, to an apartment in Shenyang, and he started looking for real estate investments to renew his fortune.

Shenyang is a sprawling industrial and financial center, the largest city in northeastern China, with a reputation as the region's crime capital. The city was overrun with violent gangs and controlled by corrupt public officials who were regularly purged by the government in Beijing, only to be replaced by new ones. The developers Hongwei knew in Shenyang were all gangsters, and when they weren't making shady deals, they were spending their nights in private gambling parlors. Hongwei would drag me along to these smoky, sleazy clubs where I would watch him play dice and roulette games. He thought I was lucky for him, but he lost hundreds of times more than he won. As winter turned to spring, Hongwei gave up his businesses completely and became obsessed with a Chinese numbers and lottery game called Mark 6. Before long, he was losing the equivalent of $1,000 to $4,500 a day. Hongwei was so addicted to gambling that he didn't eat, or sleep, or care about anything else. He would disappear for days, then return with drunken friends who took drugs that made them crazy and used prostitutes right in our apartment. If I complained about it, Hongwei would get very violent.

Once again, my mother and I were in a desperate situation. Hongwei was giving us less than 10 yuan, or $1.30, a week to buy food, and we were both dangerously thin and malnourished. My mother had developed a throat infection and I couldn't take her to a doctor. For me, the breaking point came when we were taking a walk through the city and I couldn't even give her water to ease her throat because a bottled drink cost almost 40 cents in Shenyang. We could not go on like this any longer, and we both knew the only solution available to us.

"You have to sell me, Yeonmi-ya," my mother said. "Please. I want to be sold. I'm just a burden to you here."

I felt like such a failure. I'd made a deal with Hongwei to save my family, and look at what had become of us: my sister was still missing, my father was dead, and my mother was starving. I couldn't even think about what had become of me, and I didn't care. Hongwei wanted me to bear children for him, but I could not let that happen. There was no way I would have my rapist's baby. Yet I had no idea what birth control was; we didn't have it in North Korea. So I did what had to be done when the first signs of sickness began. In China there are medicines you can swallow to stop what has been started. Afterward I felt dead inside, and perhaps I was. But I never imagined that things could get worse. And now it had come to this: I was ready to sell my own mother.

I searched and searched for a good place for her, but everyone was afraid of the police. I put out the word among the women we had sold before, and one of them called me with a prospect. There was a farm family with an unmarried son in a village several hours' drive west, past Chaoyang. Hongwei agreed with the plan—he had no use for my mother—and we went to meet the family. They seemed like kind people, the work wouldn't be too hard, and there would be plenty for my mother to eat. The family also promised to let her stay in touch with me. So we sold her to them for about $2,850.

Hongwei gambled away all the money as soon as we got back to Shenyang.

Now I was separated from my mother again, and miserable. Hongwei was broke and frustrated and taking it out on me. But as depressed as I was, I realized that there was a force inside me that would not give up. Maybe it was just anger, or maybe it was an inexplicable sense that my life might mean something someday. I had no word in my vocabulary for "dignity," or the concept of morality. I just knew what felt wrong, and what I would not accept. This situation was something I could no longer accept. I had to find a way out.

There was a large population of North Korean refugees in Shenyang. Most of them were in hiding, but some had managed to get Chinese identification cards to pass themselves off as ethnic-Korean citizens. An ID was the key to getting a job and living without fear, so I started asking Hongwei's friends if they knew where I could get one. Even Hongwei realized I had to start taking care of myself, and he agreed to give me some independence.

One of his gangster friends named Li had a fake ID made for me, but it was such poor quality that it didn't fool anyone. Then one day I had lunch at a Korean restaurant with Li and a gangster couple, and I told them my predicament. The girlfriend said she knew some people who might help me get a real ID, or at least a convincing forgery.

After lunch, the gangster's girlfriend walked with me to a very fancy place filled with rich-looking people. It was a kind of private club or restaurant, because there was food being served to men in expensive suits who sat in comfortable leather chairs. I was amazed to see a dozen very tall, beautiful young women in elegant dresses sitting next to the men.

The girlfriend seemed to know a lot of people there and said hello to them as she led me over to a table where a conservatively dressed man in his early forties was sitting alone. In fact, he was the only man in the room without a woman by his side. But everybody in the place seemed to know this man and spoke to him with respect.

"This girl is from North Korea and she wants to work, but she needs an ID," she said.

"Sit down," he said, gesturing to a chair beside him. I sat. He called himself Huang, although I don't know if that was his real name.

"Have you ever been here before?" Huang asked me. I told him it was my first time. He checked my hands and arms for track marks and tattoos that might show I was a prostitute. There were none.

"Do you drink or smoke?"

"No," I said.

"Good," he said. "You should never drink or smoke." He called the waiters and the managers and even the tall, sexy ladies over to the table to ask them if I worked there, and they all said no.

"This is a bad place for you," the man said. "You don't want to end up like those girls."

"I just want an ID so I can get a job in a restaurant," I told him.

"I have some people in the police, and I might be able to help you," he said casually. It was a life-and-death issue for me, but he made it sound like it was no big deal to him.

I told him I would be grateful for his help.

He asked me if I wanted to go sit in a park where it was quiet, to talk some more. He seemed so nice and polite that I couldn't see any problem with that, so I agreed. All I can say is that I should have known better, but somehow I still had trust in people. I had been taught to believe lies all my life, and it had become a dangerous habit.

The car that was waiting for him in the parking lot looked like a tank, with a row of lights over the cab and a custom-built bed behind the seats.

"What do you think of it?" he asked. "There are only a few of these in China."

We drove to a huge public park in the north of the city, where we sat in the car and talked.

"Tell me about yourself," he said. "How old are you?"

I was only fourteen but I told him I was eighteen, which is how old you need to be to get an ID in China.

"Do you have any family?" he asked.

"I have a mother," I said, "and I'm trying to find my sister. That's why I need an ID card to work."

"How about a boyfriend?"

"There's a man who takes care of me, but we are becoming more independent."

"Then you'll need an apartment," he said. "I have lots of them in the city. In fact, there is one right across from this park. You could stay there while you're waiting to get your ID. Do you want to see it?"

Huang drove me to one of the most luxurious buildings in Shen-yang. His huge twenty-seventh-floor apartment looked like a mu-seum. He told me he was a big art and antiques dealer who came from humble beginnings and now was one of the richest and most powerful men in Shenyang. I later found out that he had never finished elementary school and could barely write his name. But he seemed so sophisticated to me. Not like a gangster at all.

His apartment was decorated with paintings, antique ivory Buddhas, and porcelain vases covering every surface. He pointed out an elaborately carved wooden chair that he said was worth about $650,000.

There were guards in the lobby and a security system that sounded an alarm if you tried to go out on the balcony or opened the wrong door. It was like a fortress.

"If you'll stay here, I'll get you your card. I'll take care of everything for you."

At first I was very grateful to Huang. I called my mother and told her I was in a good situation with someone who would get me an ID. Hongwei kept leaving messages, but I told him not to worry. And for a short time it seemed like everything would work out fine.

The next day, Huang picked me up in his car and took me to his antiques shop. Then he took me to a friend's giant apartment to watch him play golf at an indoor putting range. He took me to visit his mother's grave, and then to an old fortune-teller who told him I would bring good luck. The fortune-teller saw a son in my palms.

"There's something special about you," Huang told me. "I want you to have this son with me."

I didn't know what to say. I knew that it was time for me to try to get away from this man, but I didn't know how because now he wouldn't let me out of his sight.

We drove to another luxury apartment building on the other side of town, and he brought me to an apartment where seven beautiful young women were living.

"See, if you stay with me, you'll have plenty of friends," he said. "You won't be lonely."

Most of the girls were in their teens, but I was the youngest by far. One of them was going to college and had her books out to study. Huang stretched out in a comfortable chair, and while some of the girls began massaging his hands and his feet, I took the opportunity to follow one of the other ones into the kitchen.

"I don't want to be here," I whispered to her. "Can you help me escape?"

"Are you insane?" she said. "Why would you want to do that? This man is rich and he's generous."

That night Huang took me back to his art-filled apartment. While he was in another room, I took out my cell phone and called my mother again.

"I don't think this is a good place for me, *Umma*," I said in Korean. "Something's wrong with this guy. He has women massaging him and he says he wants me to have his baby because he's been lucky in everything in life except having a son. . . ."

The next thing I knew, Huang was standing next to me. I don't think he understood what I was saying, but he must have read my tone of voice because he grabbed the phone out of my hand.

"You have nothing to worry about," he told my mother in Chinese. "I'm going to get your daughter an ID, and I'll send you money every month. It will all be fine." She still didn't speak the language, so she didn't really understand what was going on except that I was being kidnapped.

Huang hung up and put my phone in his pocket.

Then he grabbed me. I pulled away.

"No, that's not what I want," I said. "I want to work."

Suddenly his voice went cold.

"Do you know what they do to defectors when they are sent back to North Korea?" he said. "They string them together with wire, through the muscle on the top of their shoulders, so they can't run away. I could have you sent back tonight. Or I could have you killed and nobody would ever know what happened to you."

He tried to grab me again, and I bit him. He hit me across the face so hard that blood seeped from my mouth.

Then he stepped back.

"You know, I don't have to do this," he said. "I can have any girl I want. They all love me, even university girls. And I'm going to make you want me, too."

At that he left me alone in his apartment and locked the door.

All I could think about was getting out of that place. I didn't escape from North Korea to be this man's slave, a trophy like something in his jewel collection. Hongwei was bad, but at least he had a human heart. This man had ice in his veins, like a reptile. I had never met anyone so terrifying.

All night I kept testing the doors, but the alarms went off and the guards came running. I was kidnapped, and nobody knew where I was.

The next day, Huang returned and tried a different tactic. He brought me beautiful clothes and jewelry and told me to try them on. "Tell me what you want, and I'll buy it for you," he said.

"I want you to let me go," I said.

"No, you're going to beg for me by the time I am finished with you."

I don't know how long I was with this kidnapper. It might have been a week, maybe longer.

I was watched constantly. When I wasn't with Huang, I was under the eyes of his mistresses. I felt as trapped as I had ever been in my life. Just like in North Korea, I lived with a fear so deep and heavy that it could fill up the night sky and pin my soul to the ground with its weight. I could see no way out.

Huang didn't try to rape me again, but he could be very cruel and rough. When I refused to eat, he tried to force the food down my throat. He would threaten me, then suddenly be nice again. I thought I would never get away from him alive.

Then one day when I was sitting with a group of his mistresses in Huang's main antiques shop, Hongwei's friend Li walked in the door. Huang came out of his office to see who it was.

"Hello, big brother Huang," he said. "It's an honor to meet you."

"How do you know who I am?" Huang asked.

"Who would not know your name?" Li said. Then he gestured in my direction. "This girl's mother misses her. And I've been sent with a message from Hongwei. He wants her back, too."

"Tell Hongwei she doesn't need him anymore," Huang said. "Isn't that right, girl?"

He looked at me, and I nodded yes. I was afraid he was going to kill us all, including Hongwei and my mother, if I hesitated.

"Tell him how well I've been treating you," he said.

"He's been treating me very well," I told Hongwei's friend.

Huang told him to go.

A short time later, my cell phone rang in Huang's pocket, where he had been keeping it to monitor my calls. When he saw it was Hongwei, he answered.

Hongwei had been turning Shenyang inside out looking for me. He was frantic when he finally got in touch with my mother, and she helped him track me down. He later told me what he'd said to Huang.

"Give her back or we go to war," Hongwei said. "You can have it either black or white. If you want to play with police, I'll bring the police. If you want to play with gangs, I'll bring the gangs."

"Do you really want to make this a big deal because of one girl?" Huang said.

"No, the question is do you want to die for her and leave all that money behind?" said Hongwei.

After that phone call, Huang took me back to the apartment that was protected by guards and alarms. I knew what Hongwei was capable of doing, but I also knew this kidnapper well enough to believe that he could not let Hongwei win. So I decided to try another approach. "I can see how wrong I was," I told Huang. "I don't want to go back to Hongwei. You are a much bigger man. And why should you get into a war with him? He has nothing to lose, and you have everything at stake. I'll tell him I don't want him anymore."

I convinced the dealer that all I wanted to do was to see my mother again. "I've been so miserable only because I miss her so much," I said.

I knew that even though this man was a ruthless criminal, he was also a devout Buddhist and he had loved his mother. "Please let me go and see my mother one more time. She lives in Chaoyang. After that, I'll come back to you and we'll forget about Hongwei."

I made him believe me. The next day, he offered to send me to Chaoyang with one of his drivers, but I said no, he could just put me on the bus. It was easier. He was so convinced that he had won me over that he agreed. He even gave me back my cell phone.

As soon as the bus pulled out of the terminal, I called Hongwei.

Hongwei met me at the bus station in Chaoyang. He cried when he saw me.

"Oh, my Yeonmi-ya. What were you thinking?" he sobbed. "You don't understand how the world works."

He drove me to the farm where my mother lived. Nobody else

knew where she was, and he thought I would be safe there when Huang came looking for me.

It occurred to me that Hongwei missed me only when I had been stolen from him. And I was amazed that he would risk going to war with such a rich and powerful man just to get me back. I think it may have surprised Hongwei, too. He later told me he had never risked anything for love before.

The kind farm family welcomed me and let me live with my mother. We might have stayed for quite a while except that it was now July 2008, and the Beijing Olympics were about to begin in early August. Police had been going house to house in neighboring villages, looking for illegals. We heard of several North Korean women who had already been deported. Our Chinese family was worried that someone in town would inform on us and their farm would also be raided. So we called Hongwei, who arranged for us to hide in the town where my father was buried. But we were quickly recognized there as North Korean refugees, so Hongwei moved us again to his hometown of Chaoyang. We all lived together for a while, but we had no money. During this time my mother called the cell phone number of our friend Myung Ok, the woman who kept running away from her Chinese husband. Myung Ok was back in Shenyang, she said. And she had a job.

"What kind of job?" my mother asked.

"Nothing too strange," Myung Ok said. "If you come to Shenyang, I'll introduce you to my boss."

My mother and I were desperate again. And we were constantly changing apartments, not only to stay ahead of the police, but also because Hongwei was sure he was being haunted by my father's ghost.

At first, my father came to him in nightmares. But recently Hongwei would walk into the apartment when it was empty and find my father making something in the rice cooker. Or my father would just be sitting on the bed, staring at the wall. Hongwei cried and told me he knew my father could never forgive him for what he had done to me. And now he knew he had to let me go. He told me he regretted taking my innocence and was sorry for all the times he hurt me, although he knew it was too late for that. But he promised he would always watch out for me, and he would honor my father's spirit and tend his grave for the rest of his life.

I had such complicated feelings for this man. I had hated him for so long and I didn't think I could ever forgive him, but my heart was not so hard anymore. He was not all bad. And he had been a miracle for me, really. He had brought my mother back, brought my father to China, and helped me bury him there. I know he had tried hard to find my sister, too.

When we lived together, he had bought me lots of gold jewelry, and I had kept it hidden all this time. Now I gave it back to him. He needed it more than I did. In a way I was buying my own freedom.

I thanked him for all he had done for me, and then I said good-bye.

My mother and I took the next bus to Shenyang.

Seventeen

Like Bread from the Sky

When my mother and I arrived at Myung Ok's apartment in Shenyang, she finally told us about the job she could get for us. All we had to do, she said, was talk to men on a computer.

Myung Ok worked for a Chinese boss, or *laoban*, who rented several apartments equipped with computer terminals and Internet connections. The *laoban* was a small-time operator who worked for a bigger crime boss in Shenyang's adult chat-room underworld. At the bottom of the chain were North Korean women who had run out of choices. The women lived in small bedrooms where they could "chat" online around the clock. The customers—almost all South Korean men—searched different sites for women they liked, and then they paid by the minute to type questions and watch the women online. Most of the women took off their clothes for the men, but some just teased them into sexy conversations. The goal was to keep them online for as long as possible while their credit cards were charged for the time. The *laoban*s pocketed most of the money.

I had never even heard of a webcam before; to my mother and me, this seemed like an very strange way to make a living. I tried first to find work in a restaurant, but it was impossible to get a job without an ID. The police had been raiding places, checking for illegals. Our options for employment were extremely limited. I was still only fourteen, but I had seen all kinds of ugly things people would do to survive—and many of them were much worse than an adult chat room. As bad as my situation had been, at least Hongwei never drugged me or passed me around to other men. And compared with what might become of my mother and me once we no longer had his protection, the chat room seemed like an easy choice.

It wasn't a great job by any means, but at least you didn't have to have sex with anyone. Nobody owned you, and there was the potential to make good money. My plan was to work for long enough to pay for a good ID card; once I had an ID, I could get a better job and take care of my mother.

Shortly after we started working, Myung Ok, who was incredibly clever and resourceful, left the Chinese boss to buy her own chat-room franchise. She offered us a better deal, so we followed her.

The technology was very primitive by today's standards, but it was still baffling to us. My mother and I had never seen a computer before, so we had to learn how to type characters and watch them come up on the screen.

My mother struggled. When a customer would start a conversation, it took her so long to find the keys to type "Hello" that, by the time she looked up again, the screen would be blank and the customer gone.

"Let me do it, *Umma*," I told her. Even though it also took me a long time to type, my customers didn't seem to mind the wait. They also accepted it when I refused to take off my clothes. All I let them see was my face, and if they got too crude or insistent, I would just switch them off. It worked for me, and the men were curious to find out more about me. I would usually just type what they wanted to hear, but I also got to know some of the guys and had real conversations with them. My chat room got very popular, and sometimes I had men from six or seven Web sites calling in to my screen at the same time. I had to try not to mix them up and answer the wrong man's questions.

The more I worked, the more money I could make. If I stayed online all the time, I could earn about 4,000 yuan—more than $500—a month after the bosses took their 70 percent.

Finally, my mother and I had enough rice to eat, and we weren't afraid of being raped every night. But we were not free. The chat room was just another kind of prison. If we left the apartment, we had to look over our shoulders constantly to make sure we weren't recognized. I don't know which possibility terrified me more: falling into the hands of the Chinese police, or running into Huang or one of his people. I knew he was still looking for me, and Huang was not the kind of man you double-crossed without paying for it.

Near our apartment building there was a local middle school. From our window, I could look out and see girls my own age carrying school bags and playing with their friends. I asked my mother, "*Umma*, when can I be like that?" She had no way of responding.

I thought life would continue like this forever until my mother met a North Korean woman named Hae Soon, who was living with a South Korean man in Shenyang. Before we met Hae Soon, my mother and I had never considered escape to South Korea a possibility. But Hae Soon knew all about it and told us that the South Koreans would welcome us as citizens and help us find jobs and a place to live. She also knew how dangerous it was to try to escape from China. If you were captured and returned to North Korea, then your life would be over. Looking for work in China was a crime, but escaping to South Korea was high treason, and you would either be sent to a political prison camp, from which there is no escape, or maybe just executed.

Hae Soon told us that she knew a way out of China that had worked for others. There were Christian missionaries in the city of Qingdao who could get you through China to Mongolia, which was supposed to welcome North Korean refugees. Once you got to Mongolia, the South Korean embassy would take care of you. Hae Soon wanted to go to Qingdao and start the journey, but she didn't have the courage to do it alone. So she asked my mother and me to go with her.

As soon as I heard this woman's story, I knew we had to get to Mongolia. My mother was very afraid. We had a good thing in Shenyang, she said. It was too risky to leave, she said, and she tried to talk me out of it. But I felt an old hunger burning in me, one that told me there was more to life than just surviving. I didn't know what would happen to us, but I knew I would rather die than live like this anymore—I knew in my heart that I deserved to be treated like a person, not a hunted animal. Once again, I grabbed my mother's hands and wouldn't let go until she agreed to come with me to Mongolia.

Hae Soon gave us the cell phone number of a missionary contact. When my mother called him, he told her that he was also a North Korean defector, and because of God's mercy his life was blessed and he had found freedom. She told him about our hopes to escape to South Korea, and how we were trying to find my sister, who might already be there waiting for us. He told her that God is almighty, and he could do everything. If we prayed to God, then everything would be fine. He gave her a number to call in Qingdao. The people there would teach us more about God, and they could help us to find a way to go to South Korea.

When my mother told me about the conversation, neither of us had a clue as to what the missionary was talking about. North Korea is an atheistic country, so this was the first time we had heard anything about this Christian God. But we were willing to believe something new if it meant surviving. And the idea of mercy sounded good to us. Once again, without having much information, my mother and I decided to take a big leap.

Money was the only obstacle. We had collected some savings, but we would need more for this escape.

I can't explain why, but when I was hungry, I always believed that if I wished hard enough, bread would somehow fall from the sky. My father had the same kind of optimism despite the odds against him. But you need more than optimism and hard work to succeed. You also need luck. And maybe that old fortune-teller was right, because despite everything that has happened to me, I have been very lucky in my life.

As we prepared our escape, a friend I had met online suddenly made it all possible. He was a professional in his late thirties who lived in South Korea, and he had become one of my regulars in the chat room. Most of the men I met online thought I was somewhere in Seoul because I lied to them. But this man was different. He treated me like a real person, so I told him some of my real story. He was so moved that he wanted to help me escape. He flew up to Shenyang to meet me and gave me enough money to cover our expenses. All he wanted, he said, was for me to give him a call once we made it to the South, although I doubt he expected even that. He was a lonely man with a good heart.

Soon we were set to go. My mother asked Myung Ok if she wanted to come with us, but she had her own business, and she was too afraid to leave.

By early February, it was time to leave Shenyang. The dangerous escape weighed heavily on our minds. I bought myself a brown tweed coat to wear on our journey, and we decided to splurge on one last, big meal at a Korean restaurant—something we would never do under ordinary circumstances. We even went out to a karaoke bar—the ordinary kind that's just for fun with friends.

I'm not much of a singer, but I've always loved my mother's voice. When I was young, she sang to me while she was cleaning the house or putting me to sleep. Her voice was the most beautiful, warmest sound I'd ever known. Hearing her sing again broke down a wall I had built around my heart. For nearly two years, I'd felt like all five of my senses were numbed. I could not feel, smell, see, hear, or taste the world around me. If I had allowed myself to experience these things in all their intensity, I might have lost my mind. If I had allowed myself to cry, I might never have been able to stop. So I survived, but I never felt joy, never felt safe. Now, as I listened to my mother sing the old songs, that numbness melted away. I was overwhelmed by the boundless love I felt for her, and also the intense fear of losing her. That sense of dread hollowed out my chest like a physical pain. She was everything to me. She was all I had.

Now I had to be true to the promise I'd made my father, to keep her safe and find Eunmi. That meant getting us to South Korea.

Eighteen

Following the Stars

The next morning, my mother and I and Hae Soon began a long, tense bus ride from Shenyang to Qingdao. It was about 750 miles by road, and at any point the bus could have been boarded by Chinese police checking IDs. But our luck was good, and we made it to the city in two days without being searched.

Qingdao is a huge, modern port located just across the Yellow Sea from South Korea. From there a traveler with a passport could fly to Seoul's Incheon airport in just over an hour. But North Korean defectors have to take a much more tortuous route to freedom.

We were met at the Qingdao bus station by a middle-aged ethnic Korean woman who took us to an apartment building in a nondescript neighborhood. There we were dropped off in one of at least two shelters maintained in the city by a clandestine Protestant mission. It was the first stop in an underground railroad, where North Korean defectors were trained in the Bible while they waited for their chance to escape through Mongolia. The mission was run by a South Korean pastor with help from the ethnic Korean woman and a Han Chinese Christian man who organized and guided the dangerous trips to the Mongolian border.

The People's Republic of China has had a complicated, often violent relationship with organized religion. Churches were purged during the Cultural Revolution of the 1960s, although in the more recent era of economic reforms, the atheistic government has allowed some churches to operate openly. But Christian missions that proselytize to nonbelievers are illegal, and so is helping North Koreans escape to other countries. We were told that if the authorities found out about the Qingdao mission, the pastor and his helpers could be sent to prison and we would be deported. For this reason we were never told the real names of our rescuers.

Our party of three from Shenyang shared a small apartment with eight or nine other female North Korean defectors. We were warned not to make too much noise and never to leave the apartment by ourselves—although some people did anyway. We were each expected to buy our own food on a stipend of 5 yuan—about 65 cents—a day. Once a week, the ethnic Korean lady would take us someplace safe to shop. Luckily, my mother and I had money to buy more food, which we shared with our group.

When we arrived, my mother and I had never heard of Jesus Christ. We got some help from one of the other defectors who explained it this way: "Just think of God as Kim Il Sung and Jesus as Kim Jong Il. Then it makes more sense."

I have to confess that I was just going along with it at first. If I had to accept Christ as my savior to get to South Korea, then I was going to be the best Christian these people had ever seen. We had to worship every morning and then study the Bible all day. The pastor had us write out page after page from the book of Proverbs in Korean. We did a lot of singing and praying and repenting for our sins. I had no trouble grasping the concept of an all-powerful, all-knowing God. It was a lot like what we had been taught in North Korea about our Dear Leader, who knew everything and would take care of everything for us if we were loyal to him. But I had trouble understanding how He was a merciful God. I wondered why this God existed in South Korea but not in North Korea.

But before long, I was swept up in the songs and the spirit of the gospel and lent myself completely to the message of hope. I also found that I was very good at prayer.

S oon after we arrived, my mother called our friend Sun Hi, who was living in a nearby province with her Chinese "husband" and her nine-year-old daughter, Hyong Sim. We had lived together briefly in one of Hongwei's apartments, and Sun Hi and my mother had bonded instantly. They were the same age, both from Hyesan (although they didn't know each other there), and both were searching for their older daughters who had disappeared in China's network of traffickers. Sun Hi's life had been complicated and tragic, but she was a resilient, even buoyant, woman, and we had come to think of her and Hyong Sim as family.

My mother told Sun Hi about our plans and how she could also escape to South Korea if she contacted the mission. Sun Hi and her young daughter were having a hard time surviving on her husband's poor farm, so she was eager for the chance to leave. She and Hyong Sim arrived in Qingdao in mid-February and joined our group.

Unfortunately, we were already making preparations to switch to another apartment. My mother was having trouble getting along with Hae Soon, who had a controlling personality. My mother's intoler-

ance might have simply been caused by stress, but she found it unbearable to live in the same apartment with Hae Soon, and she didn't want
to continue our journey with her. We made some thank-you offerings
to the ethnic Korean woman to help support the mission and within a
short time were moved to another, similar apartment with a different
group who were also preparing for their departure. This happened to
be the next team scheduled to leave for Mongolia, so we also would
be getting out of China sooner than the others.

Our new group included my mother, myself, and three other
women—one who had lived in China for almost a decade, one who
was in her early twenties, and one who was my mother's age. There
was also a young family: a father, mother, and a boy of about three.
The family had relatives in South Korea who paid a lot of money to
send a broker to get them in North Korea. They went directly from
the border to the mission in Qingdao, so they had never lived in China
and didn't understand a word of Chinese.

My mother and I liked these people, and we fit in well with the
group. They had finished their Bible training, and the pastor thought
we were all ready to go.

Then one day in late February, as we were making our final preparations to leave, the pastor called a prayer meeting with our new
group. This is where we praised the Lord and repented our sins,
which seemed like a familiar ritual to anyone from North Korea. We
sat in a circle and criticized ourselves and begged God for forgiveness
for all we had done wrong.

We had done it many times with this pastor, but this time felt
different. After I repented, the pastor said, "Don't you have more to
tell?"

I looked at him curiously. He turned to my mother. "Surely there
are more sins you can tell us about?"

We were shocked. My mother and I communicated silently with

our eyes. We could only imagine that someone in the other group had told the pastor about our work in the chat room.

"We repented our sins privately with God," my mother said. "Do we have to say it in front of everyone?"

He told us yes, we had to make a full confession in front of everyone and beg for forgiveness.

We started crying, and at that point he asked everybody else to leave the room.

My mother and I told him that we had worked in the chat rooms in Shenyang, but we were so sorry, we only did it to survive. We thought God had forgiven us.

The pastor shook his head gravely.

"No, you are sinners. And I cannot allow you to go to Mongolia in a sinful state. You will put all the innocent ones at risk."

We begged and begged the pastor, promising him that we would never do such a sinful thing ever again. We were so, so sorry. Couldn't he forgive us?

"It's not up to me," he said. "You have to pray to God to forgive you."

Then my mother said, "You're so right. We were too sinful, and if our deep repentance was not enough for God to forgive us, then we don't dare go with the others and bring them harm. We can only say how sorry we are and ask for mercy."

The pastor didn't say anything for a while. Then he read us a passage from Isaiah, translated into Korean:

"'Come now, let us settle the matter,' says the Lord. 'Though your sins are like scarlet, they shall be as white as snow; though they are red as crimson, they shall be like wool.'"

The words soothed me, and I thanked the pastor again and again for his prayers. But I left the meeting feeling dirty and ashamed for what I had done to survive.

. . .

The next day, the ethnic Korean woman told my mother and me that we could go with the team.

The pastor came to the apartment one more time to pray with us before we left for Mongolia and to wish us a safe journey. He pulled me aside for some final words. "Please live a *proper* life in South Korea," he said. I could tell his expectations for me were not good—he thought my past would shape my future. How could I tell him that all I wanted was to live and be free?

Our group was planning to cross the border into Mongolia at night, on foot, during one of the coldest times of the year, when temperatures in that part of the Gobi Desert can drop to minus-27 degrees Fahrenheit. Winter crossings were supposed to be safer because the Chinese border patrols were lighter and they wouldn't be expecting anyone to risk freezing to death during such a dangerous trek. But there was still a real possibility that we would be arrested before we got to the border. And in that case, my mother and I had decided we were not going to be taken. My mother had stashed away a large cache of sleeping pills—the same kind my grandmother had used to kill herself. I hid a razor blade in the belt of my tweed jacket so that I could slit my own throat before they sent me back to North Korea.

The night before we left, I called Hongwei. We had not seen each other in months, and I still had such complicated feelings for him. But now that I was facing my death, I was more at peace with my past. I had spent too much energy and time hating and being intolerant of the choices others had made. Now, at age fifteen, I felt that there was not enough time left to express my love and gratitude to the people in my life. I told Hongwei that I had prayed for my father to stop haunting him and to forgive him. I prayed that I could forgive him, too. I also wanted him to know I was escaping through Mongolia, because if I died in the desert, he would be the only one who remembered me.

By the end of our conversation I was crying, and Hongwei's voice was choked with emotion.

"Good-bye, Yeonmi-ya," he said. "I wish only the best for you. Please stay alive."

For once, he got what he wished for.

I t took four long days to reach the border. Our band of defectors traveled by train and bus, accompanied by the Han Chinese man who worked for the mission. He was of normal height, and he looked to be in his late forties, just an average-looking Chinese guy, which helped him avoid attention while he was escorting undocumented defectors out of the country. He didn't speak any Korean, and I spoke the best Mandarin Chinese in our group, so I had to translate as he told us what to do if we were stopped by police. "If any of you gets captured, please don't give up the rest of the team," he said. "Tell the police you were traveling alone, and save the rest of us."

Naturally, we were all on edge as we boarded the train in Qingdao. We rode all day, pretending to be asleep so that nobody would talk to us. In Beijing, we switched to a bus, and our route wound through the mountains where ancient Chinese emperors had built a meandering chain of great stone walls to keep out the tribal armies of the northern steppe. The land grew flatter and emptier as we made our way along a two-lane highway into the high desert of Inner Mongolia. We were traveling without possessions except for small backpacks for bottled water, snacks, and a few personal items, which we clutched nervously in our laps as we scanned the highway for signs of roadblocks and checkpoints. Thankfully, there were none.

The long ride ended at Erlian, a tiny dust-blown border town in the middle of the vast Gobi Desert. We arrived very early in the morning, and our guide started searching for a place to hide until evening. But everywhere we went we were turned away because we didn't have proper identification. Finally, we found a guesthouse that would accept cash and not ask questions.

We spent an uneasy day in our room while we waited for night to fall. My mother and I were very suspicious of the couple who ran the guesthouse, and even though it was freezing cold, we kept the window open in our room so that we could jump out quickly if we heard the police coming. As the sun was starting to set, our guide told us he would be dropping us off close to the border and then we'd have to carry on alone. Because the little boy's father was the only man on our team, he was put in charge of leading us through the desert. The ethnic Korean woman at the mission had given us two flashlights and two compasses, and the guide showed the father how to find a setting. We were to walk in a northwest direction from the drop site, then pass through five barbed-wire fences before arriving at a very tall fence that meant we had reached the border. We should identify ourselves as North Korean refugees to the first person we saw in Mongolia, and turn ourselves in to be rescued. If nobody came, we should find the railroad tracks and follow them to the nearest town.

At least that was the way it was supposed to work.

A taxi pulled up in the night and drove us to a construction site a few miles outside of town. The parents of the little boy had spoken to him to make sure he didn't cry and give away our position as he was carried through the desert. Luckily, he was a good child and didn't make a sound, although we had sedatives ready if he needed them.

Our Chinese guide gave us some last-minute instructions while I translated them into Korean: "If you look out in the desert, the bright lights are coming from a town on the Mongolian side," he said. "Head toward them. The lights from the town on the Chinese side are much dimmer. Stay away from them."

Above us, a quarter moon hung in a sky blazing with stars. Our guide pointed to the brightest star of all.

"If you get separated from the group, or can't use your compass, just look up and find the star. That will be north."

Then he sent us on our way. After we had walked a few steps, my mother and I looked back and saw that he had dropped to his knees on the frozen ground. He had clutched his hands together and was lifting them toward the sky. I wondered: *Why does this person, who doesn't even speak our language, care so much about us that he is willing to risk his life for us?* It moved us both to tears. I said a silent prayer of thanks as we became a part of the night.

There was no cover anywhere, no trees or even bushes—just miles upon endless miles of featureless sand and stone dotted with clumps of dried grass. The cold was like a living thing, stalking us as we walked. It clawed heavily at my skin and grabbed at my legs to slow them. I immediately regretted wearing the tweed wool coat I had bought in Shenyang instead of a parka. The missionaries had told us to travel light for this journey, but I had taken them too literally. I hadn't even brought gloves and a scarf. I leaned against my mother for warmth, and she gave me her heavy coat when I couldn't stop shivering. My mother's shoes were too thin for the rough terrain, and she kept stumbling. So the baby's father gave my mother an extra pair of running shoes to wear. They were too big, but she tied the laces very tight to keep them on her feet. I doubt she would have made it without his help.

I t was the longest night of my life. Every time we heard a noise or saw a headlight in the distance, we panicked. After we had wriggled under the fourth barbed-wire fence, we heard the sound of engines in the distance, then we saw a huge searchlight sweeping over the desert. We threw ourselves to the ground and tried not to move. The boy's father had been given a brand new cell phone for the journey, and he used it to call the mission in Qingdao. Could the pastor tell us whether the searchlight belonged to the Chinese or the Mongolians? And what should we do?

The pastor's answer was "Don't get arrested."

We stayed on the ground and prayed until the sounds and the light faded into the distance. Now we were afraid to turn on the flashlight to look at the compass, so we used the stars to guide us as we walked and crawled through the desert. After we crossed the fifth barbed-wire fence, I thought our ordeal might be over soon. But then some clouds covered the stars, and we lost our bearings. For a while we may have been walking in circles until we came up with a plan: all of us huddled around the boy's father to block the flashlight while he read the compass to find the right direction.

As the hours went on, it got colder and colder, and I started doubting that any of us would make it. I thought about dying out here in the desert. Would anyone find my bones or mark my grave? Or would I be lost and forgotten, as if I had never existed? To realize I was completely alone in this world was the scariest thing I've felt in my life, and the saddest.

I also started hating the dictator Kim Jong Il that night. I hadn't thought that much about it before, but now I blamed him for our suffering. I finally allowed myself to think bad thoughts about him because even if he could read my mind, I was probably going to die out here anyway. What could he do, kill me again? But even in the face of death, betraying the Dear Leader was probably the hardest thing I had ever done. I was beyond the reach of his revenge, yet it felt like his hand was following me everywhere I went, trying to pull me back. My mother later told me she was thinking the same thing as we staggered through the night.

Just when I thought it couldn't get worse, a pack of wild animals surrounded us in the darkness. I heard them scratching and panting as they passed by, and I could see the faint glow of their eyes reflecting the dim moonlight. I don't know if they were goats or wolves, but I completely lost my mind.

"Help us! Is anybody out there? Anybody!" I screamed. At that point I didn't care if it was Chinese or Mongolians.

But there was no one at all.

I was ready to give up, to lie down and die. I couldn't walk another step. I had started hallucinating hours ago, seeing wire fences on the horizon. "*Umma*, look!" I said over and over again. But when we reached the spot, nothing would be there.

Just before dawn, it got so cold that we were afraid we would all freeze to death. Out of desperation, we built a small fire with whatever dried twigs and grasses that we could glean from the desert. But the fire wasn't big enough. We were discussing burning some of our extra clothes for fuel when suddenly we heard a train approaching. It sounded close, even though we thought we were miles out in the wilderness. But in the cold, heavy air, the sound seemed to be coming from two different places. Most of our group ran one way, but my mother and I thought it came from somewhere else, so we ran in another direction.

Minutes later, the big border fence took shape in the half-light just ahead of us. I thought it was another mirage, but then we saw the holes in the wire and bits of cloth snagged where others had crossed before us. This was it! As we scrambled through one of the holes, the heavy barbs ripped at my pants and my coat as if they were trying to rake me back into China. My mother helped me tear myself loose, and suddenly we were free.

The sun rose behind us, casting our long faint shadows across the desert floor as we walked into Mongolia. My mother grabbed my hand and reminded me that it was March 4—my father's birthday.

PART THREE

South Korea

Nineteen

The Freedom Birds

We had been breathing the free air of Mongolia for only a few minutes when a soldier in camouflage gear ran up to us.

He raised his rifle and shouted something in a language we'd never heard before. This had to mean he was Mongolian. We were rescued!

"Xiexie! Xiexie!" I cried in Chinese. "Thank you! Thank you!"

The soldier kept shouting at us, but I was so happy to be captured that I was jumping up and down with my hands in the air. He tried to keep a straight face but he couldn't help laughing.

The mood changed quickly as the rest of our group appeared in the distance with their hands above their heads, followed by several more soldiers with their weapons leveled. When they had all of us together, the Mongolian soldiers started talking into their two-way radios all at once, and the scene became very confusing. Within a few minutes, three or four military off-road vehicles came roaring across the open desert to surround us.

A high-ranking officer rode in one of the vehicles, and all eight of us were ordered to squeeze into two rows of seats behind him. As soon as we were inside, he turned to us and said in crude Chinese, *"Hui zhongguo."* "Back to China."

I was stunned. This wasn't supposed to be happening! Without thinking, we jumped out of the vehicle. Only my mother and the father holding his son remained in their seats. The soldiers tried to push us back in, but we grabbed their uniforms, crying and begging for mercy. "Save us! Please don't send us back! They'll execute us!"

I felt for the razor I had hidden in my belt, ready to pull it out and slash my throat. I was completely serious. This was the end for me.

"We'll kill ourselves before you send us back," I cried.

"Yes, we'll die first!" screamed another woman.

The soldiers looked scared, even ashamed. Finally, one of them said, "Okay. Let's go to Seoul."

That calmed us enough to get us back into the vehicle. But we panicked again when the driver pulled away in the direction of the Chinese border post.

"No! We can't go back!" I cried. Then we all started wailing and begging again.

One of the North Korean women nudged the boy's father and said, "Pray!" He whispered back to her, "I'm praying!"

I was too shattered to remember my prayers, but the missionaries told us when we can't pray, just say a few words. In my mind, I kept repeating, "Jesus' blood is my blood." I didn't know what that meant, but it seemed appropriate, and it was all I could think of to help us survive. Obviously, I couldn't count on human beings at the moment, so I would have prayed to the rocks, trees, and sky if it would get us out of there.

All this time my mother had been trying to figure out a way to save her daughter. She thought about throwing me out the door so that I could escape before we got to China. In North Korea, a lot of people throw themselves off running trains to avoid arrest. Then she remembered that cars aren't like trains—they can stop, and I would easily be recaptured. The only real option was attempting suicide. But luckily it never came to that.

The vehicle bounced through town, past the road leading to the Chinese border post, and kept going until it turned in to a Mongolian military base.

As soon as the SUV pulled through the gates, all eight of us were escorted into a one-story building that looked like a barracks or a jail. The women were taken one by one into a room and ordered by a female soldier to take off all our clothes. She even searched our hair to see if we were carrying money or drugs there. She took all the Chinese yuan my mother had left on her. They treated us like criminals instead of refugees. Still, there was a large room with bunk beds where we could sleep, and they gave us some food. We remained at this military base for more than a week, and the soldiers would frequently tell us we were being sent back to China. We didn't know if they were serious, or just being cruel.

Once in a while, some Mongolian officers would come by to take pictures of us and ask questions, so I was called on to interpret for everyone. Except for the little boy, I was the youngest in the group, but because I could communicate with our captors, I took on the responsibility for all of us.

We were relieved when some high-ranking officers took us by train to the capital, Ulan Bator, where we transferred to another military base, and finally to a secure compound in the countryside. There were more than twenty other defectors waiting there when we arrived, and more came in as others moved out.

The men and women were divided up into two different rooms. There were no beds, just some boards piled with blankets. Once a week, the staff made hot water for us to take a bath—the men always went first, just like in North Korea. We were freezing most of the time because it was still winter, but we didn't complain. For North Koreans, this kind of place seemed normal, even luxurious, although South Koreans would probably call it a prison camp.

We could not leave, and we had to keep strict hours for sleeping, eating, and working. The adults cleaned the building, while I mostly worked keeping up the grounds outside. About once a week, some kind of representative from the South Korean embassy would come by to ask us questions and have us write down our histories. But the embassy workers couldn't tell us how long we would have to wait, or exactly what kind of a place this was.

Obviously, there was some kind of quiet agreement between Mongolia and the South Korean government to warehouse defectors at this camp until they could be flown to Seoul. Mongolia's stated policy was to allow North Korean refugees from China safe passage to a third country, but events on the ground were much murkier. In fact, defectors were caught in a long-standing political and economic tug-of-war. Once a satellite state of the Soviet Union, Mongolia was now a multiparty democracy with a growing market economy. It had diplomatic and economic ties with both North and South Korea, as well as China and the United States, and its treatment of North Korean refugees seemed to reflect the relative importance of each relationship at any given moment. In 2005, about five hundred North Koreans were coming over the border every month. By 2009, when we crossed, that number had tapered off to a trickle as China increased its border patrols and Mongolia sweetened its relationship with Pyongyang. The situation got so bad that brokers and rescue missions were now steering defectors away from Mongolia to an alternate escape route through Southeast Asia.

In fact, our band of eight North Koreans was among the last groups sent to Mongolia from the mission in Qingdao. Sun Hi arrived in Mongolia with her daughter a month after our own escape. After my mother and I jumped ahead of the queue, Sun Hi, Hyong Sim, and the troublemaker Hae Soon were all assigned to a third group that left even later than we had originally been scheduled to leave for Mongolia. This turned out to be very lucky for them—every member of our original team was captured by the Chinese before they reached the border. They were all sent back to North Korea.

Sun Hi's group departed two weeks after the original group was captured. Like us, they made it through the fence, only to be seized by Mongolian border guards who tried to send them back to China. Sun Hi actually swallowed poison before she would let them do that, and they had to rush her to a hospital to revive her. We later heard that the Qingdao mission was shut down shortly afterward. The ethnic Korean woman and our Han Chinese missionary guide were arrested and sent to Chinese prisons for the crime of helping North Koreans escape to freedom.

My mother and I didn't know how long we would be held in Mongolia, or whether we could still be sent back to China. Our hearts withered with each day of waiting. But it helped to be working outside, because then the place didn't feel so much like a prison and there were beautiful views around Ulan Bator. Sometimes my mother joined me, and we both liked to gaze at the mountains and think about being free. Several times a day, sleek silver jets flew low in the sky as they took off from an airport somewhere in the valley.

As the planes gained altitude, they looked like determined birds fly-
ing away to freedom. My mother saw me staring at them and said,
"We'll be taking a plane like that to South Korea. We'll be free soon."
I tried to imagine myself on each of them, disappearing into the sky,
but it seemed impossible to me.

On April 20, 2009, a South Korean representative picked us up
at the facility and drove us to Ulan Bator's international airport. Because we had no identification, we were given South Korean
passports with fake names on them to get us through Mongolian customs and immigration.

We were warned not to use any Korean words in the airport, so
we waited in the departure lounge in silence, afraid to even breathe.
Every time I saw a person in a military uniform, I jumped out of my
skin. (Sometimes I still have that reaction.) Finally, we were escorted
onto the jet, and I was so relieved that nobody stopped us. Of course,
it was the first time in our lives we had been on an airplane. When we
took our seats, my mother and I exchanged amazed looks, and then I
high-fived her. It was a gesture I had learned from South Korean movies, and I was ready to be a South Korean. Or so I thought.

As we waited for the plane to taxi, my mother and I held each
other's hands tightly. I felt like I was in one of those movies where all
kinds of thoughts race through your mind at a turning point in your
life. I relived every step we took in the Gobi Desert; I remembered
the frozen river we had crossed into China, and my narrow escapes
from the brokers and gangsters before we finally made it to Mongolia.
I saw my father, who had somehow been with me all this way, helping
me stay alive, guiding me through the danger. I felt so guilty that he
had died without ever tasting freedom, and now I was going without
him. I felt the shame of the survivor who lives while so many friends

and family members have died or are trapped in a living hell. But my sadness and guilt were eased by the thought of my mother's happiness, and the hope that my sister would soon be found—if she wasn't already waiting for us in South Korea.

I was sitting in a window seat, and I couldn't wait to take off so I could see the horizon and the ocean, which I had known only from pictures and videos. But as soon as we started barreling down the runway, I got a bad case of motion sickness. I kept my eyes away from the window for the rest of the three-and-a-half-hour flight, even when we started our descent to Incheon International Airport in South Korea. I didn't want to ruin my first view of freedom by being sick.

We were told to stay in our seats after we landed and to wait for everyone else to get off the plane. Then a man from the National Intelligence Service, South Korea's version of the CIA, boarded to escort us from the plane. He was soon joined by more agents to bring us through the airport. These men were so handsome and spoke with such beautiful accents, like the South Koreans I had watched on pirated videos, that my mother had to nudge my ribs to stop me from staring at them.

I stepped off the airplane onto a different planet. The first thing I saw was a cavernous white corridor bathed in brilliant light. The moving walkway rolled like a magic carpet, taking us to the main terminal. All the fancy South Korean girls gliding by in the other direction wore fine leather jackets and miniskirts and had candy-colored headphones clamped over their ears. When I saw them, I felt like crawling into a mouse hole to hide my shabby tweed coat and mended jeans. It was so embarrassing to be dressed like a poor country girl in this dazzling new place.

When the moving walkway came to an end, I was afraid to step off onto the shiny marble floor. It looked as slick as a frozen river, and I thought I would slip. Everyone waited for me as I took a trip to the public restroom. I thought I had seen modern toilets in China, but this was incomprehensible. The bowls were so shiny and clean, I thought that was where you washed your hands. And the faucets in the row of basins kept turning on mysteriously when you walked by, but then would stop unexpectedly. I was too ashamed to ask for help, and I felt very stupid and inadequate. So even before I officially entered South Korea, I felt like a failure.

The lovely NIS agents whisked all eight of us through the back corridors of the airport and onto a waiting bus.

Our first stop was a hospital, where I received the first checkup of my life. It was very strange, to be examined by doctors with so much modern equipment. But the strangest thing was being asked to pee into a cup. *What?* I had no idea how to do that. And they gave me such an awesome cup, I didn't want to use it for that!

The doctors got the results back quickly, and I was okay. No TB, no contagious diseases. Soon we were all free to go on to the next step of our journey.

The National Intelligence Center is a heavily secured, restricted facility about an hour's drive outside Seoul. As soon as we arrived, our belongings were taken away and we were given large bags filled with clothes and shampoo and other personal items for our stay. At this point, our friendly welcome was over and it became clear that this place was more like a jail than a refugee shelter. The people who processed us were rough and used very crude language, even with the children. As in Mongolia, we were each taken to a room to be stripped and thoroughly searched, which again left me feeling humiliated and violated. It was a depressing way to begin our life of freedom.

The purpose of the Center is to weed out imposters: ethnic Koreans from China trying to emigrate to South Korea, and North Korean agents disguised as defectors. It is a legitimate concern, because a few dozen defectors have been arrested for spying over the years. Yet this is a tiny fraction of the more than twenty-six thousand North Koreans who have passed through the Center and now live in South Korea.

The NIS agents explained to us that we had to be interrogated and investigated before we could enter the country. My mother and I had to decide how much of our story to tell. We were so worried after the terrible reaction from the pastor in Qingdao when he learned we had worked in a chat room. We thought that the less these South Koreans knew about our past, the better off we would be. So we tried to come up with a story that left out the fact that I had been trafficked in China when I was thirteen, or that I had lived as Hongwei's mistress. But the story was so complicated and difficult to memorize that my mother decided it was easier and better to just tell the truth. The only thing she held back was the divorce from my father. She always thought of it as fake, anyway, because they had done it only so she could change her residence while he was in prison. She wanted to honor my father by being his wife, even in death.

After we had been searched, our little team from Qingdao was led to a room filled with twenty or more newly arrived defectors who were lying around on blankets on the floor. Each of us was given a pen and paper and told to write down everything about ourselves. After we handed in our essays, we could talk, sleep, or watch a closed-circuit television that showed only the Discovery Channel dubbed in Korean or with subtitles. I learned about life on the ocean floor, desert islands, and crocodiles in Africa. I even saw for the first time how a baby grows in its mother's belly. It was a long wait, but very educational. The food was good, too. We were fed a lot of snacks and cookies, and we lined up for meals of delicious new foods like curry, which

I'd never had before. Some of the staff in the housing units were mean to us, but most of them were extremely nice and friendly. We were given a few hours each day to stretch and exercise, but other than that, we were held in isolation as people moved on to the next stage of their interrogation and new ones arrived to take their places.

We heard a lot of frightening and sorrowful stories from the people we met. We learned that another friend of Myung Ok's, who had been working in the chat room to pay for a passage through Southeast Asia, had drowned in the flooded Mekong River before she could get to Thailand. My mother and I had wanted to take that route as well, but it was too expensive for us. There was no safe way to escape from North Korea, and we were lucky to have made it out alive.

After about twenty days in the big waiting room, my mother and I were moved to a smaller room with a woman and her three children. She told us her husband had been arrested in China right in front of her, but she had to pretend she didn't know him in order to save their children. She felt so guilty for leaving him behind. My mother tried to assure her she had done the right thing, but at night the woman cried out for him in her sleep.

After two more weeks, it was finally time for our individual interrogations. My mother and I were moved into solitary rooms, each outfitted with a small bed, table, chair, and tiny bathroom. At mealtimes, someone brought the food inside the room and picked up the tray after I ate.

The agent in charge of my interrogation was tall and middle-aged, and spoke with a silky accent that I found charming at first. But a lot of the questions he asked made me feel very uncomfortable, the same way I had felt in Qingdao.

He started by questioning me about what I learned in school and other things that only North Korean children would know, like the Young Pioneer oath. He had me draw a map of my neighborhood, and he asked me about what my family did in North Korea. Sometimes I was taken to his office to answer questions, and sometimes he called me on the phone to verify something my mother had said. I know it was necessary, but it made me anxious. Especially when he wanted me to talk about China.

Toward the end of the interrogation, he asked, "Do you have any tattoos?"

I knew that he was really asking, "Were you a whore?" Prostitutes in China can often be identified by tattoos on their arms or backs. My face was burning with shame that this man felt entitled to ask such a question. What did it matter anyway? He knew my past; he knew I had worked in a chat room. Now he was looking at me like I was something he just scraped off his shoe. In his eyes I was lower than an insect.

"No, I don't have tattoos," I said.

"Are you *sure*?" he insisted.

"I don't. Why can't you believe me?"

"You know, I can bring in a woman to take off your clothes."

"Go ahead! Check it right now!"

"Okay, okay, relax," he said. "I believe you."

The agent tried to change the subject. "So what do you plan to do in South Korea?"

Without hesitating, I said, "I want to study and go to university."

He snorted with surprise and said, "Oh, I don't think you can do that." Then he added, "But I suppose everybody should get a second chance."

A second chance? I thought. *A second chance is what criminals get.* I knew I wasn't a criminal; I did what I had to do to survive and save my family. But now my heart sank. I realized I had no hope in this place. I felt dirty and lost, just like I had when the pastor was lecturing me about sin. If this was the way people were going to treat me when they found out who I was, then I would have to become somebody else. Somebody who could be accepted and succeed in South Korea. My life so far had been all about survival. I had found a way to survive in North Korea. I had found a different way to survive in China. But I wondered whether I had the energy to survive here. I felt so very tired.

I went back to my cell-like room and looked out the window at the country where I thought I would be free. All I saw was another hell. How easy it would be to run my wrist along the sharp metal sill until I cut so deep that my life would burst open like a sudden storm and end just as quickly.

But then I remembered I had a promise to keep. Like my father, I vowed that my eyes wouldn't close until I found my sister. I wanted to live to see her again.

During our escape from China, my mother and I asked everyone we met whether they had seen Eunmi. Nobody had. We gave her name to the NIS agents when we first arrived at the Center, but they had no record of her. I was crushed, but still I would not give up. If she was alive in China, all I had to do was let her know where to find us, and she would find a way to come.

By the beginning of June, our group of about 130 newly arrived defectors was ready to leave the Center. We had all been cleared by national security. The evening before we departed, the staff threw us a big party to welcome us to our new life. They wished us good luck, and they knew we would need it. Our next stop was a resettlement center where North Koreans were taught how to be South Koreans.

Twenty

Dreams and Nightmares

The first thing they taught us at the Hanawon Resettlement Center was how to sing the national anthem. We were all very good at it. After all, this was the sort of skill we North Koreans had been perfecting all our lives. The rest of the work was much harder.

Hanawon, located about forty miles south of Seoul, means "House of Unity."

The campus of redbrick buildings and green lawns surrounded by security fences was built in 1999 by South Korea's Ministry of Unification, a cabinet-level agency created to prepare for the day when North and South would somehow be reunited. Its programs are designed to help defectors transition into a modern society—something that will have to happen on a massive scale if North Korea's 25 million people are ever allowed to join the twenty-first century.

The Republic of Korea has evolved separately from the Hermit Kingdom for more than six decades, and even the language is different now. In a way, Hanawon is like a boot camp for time travelers from the Korea of the 1950s and '60s who grew up in a world without ATMs, shopping malls, credit cards, or the Internet. South Koreans use a lot of unfamiliar slang, and English has crept into the vocabulary as "Konglish." For example, a handbag in South Korea is now a *han-du-bag-u*. And shopping is *syoping*. I was amazed when I learned that people shopped for fun. There was so much more: printer, scanner, salad, hamburger, pizza, clinic. This wasn't just a new vocabulary for me; these were code words for entry into a completely new world.

It was both mystifying and exhilarating. The staff at Hanawon tried to teach us as much as they could in the three months before we were released into our new hypercompetitive, digitalized, and democratized homeland.

As soon as we arrived, our little group from Qingdao was assigned to a team—Group 129—and issued casual uniforms of track pants, T-shirts, hoodies, and running shoes to wear during our stay. The facility was designed to house two hundred defectors at a time, but during our stay it was packed with around six hundred residents—all women and children eighteen and under. Adult men were sent to a separate facility. We slept four or five to a room, and ate meals in a communal cafeteria.

While my mother and the other adults were taught how to open a bank account, use a credit card, pay rent, and register to vote, I joined the other teenagers and children in classes to prepare us for the rigorous South Korean education system. First they tested our knowledge levels. I was fifteen years old, but after missing so much school, I scored at a second-grade math level and was even worse at reading and writing.

I had to start my education over, from the beginning.

A lot of us had a hard time adjusting to the classroom. Sitting still in a chair seemed uncomfortable and unnatural. And the lessons were often baffling. Our schoolbooks no longer used "American bastards" as units for addition and subtraction—now we had cute, colorful things like apples and oranges. But I still didn't know my multiplication tables. And I needed help with basic things like the ABC alphabet. Other than Korean characters, the only alphabet I knew was the one we used to spell Russian words in North Korea. Learning a new one now seemed completely overwhelming.

The instructors spent a lot of time teaching us about the world outside the sealed borders of North Korea. It was the first time we learned that there were prosperous democracies all over the globe, and that North Korea was one of the poorest countries on the planet, and the most repressive. Every day, the instructors challenged fundamental beliefs that had been drilled into our heads from birth. Some corrections were easier to take than others. I was able to believe that Kim Jong Il lived in luxurious mansions while his people starved. But I could not accept that it was his father, the Great Leader Kim Il Sung, and not the evil Yankee and South Korean invaders, who started the Korean War in 1950. For a long time, I simply refused to believe it. Assuming that North Korea was always the victim of imperialist aggression was part of my identity. It's not easy to give up a worldview that is built into your bones and imprinted on your brain like the sound of your own father's voice. Besides, if everything I had been taught before was a lie, how could I know these people weren't lying, too? It was impossible to trust anyone in authority.

At Hanawon, we also learned some rules of the society we were about to enter. For instance, the instructors told us we couldn't beat anyone here. That would cost us a lot of money and we might end up in jail. This was shocking to the boys, but sounded very good to me. In North Korea and China there were no laws like that, and when someone hit me, I never expected them to be punished. I thought I had no choice because I was weak. So this legal system seemed very attractive to me because it protected weak people from those with more power. I'd never imagined such a concept.

I don't know if the other defectors had the same problems, but for me the most difficult part of the program was learning to introduce myself in class. Almost nobody knew how to do this, so the teachers taught us that the first thing you say is your name, age, and hometown. Then you can tell people about your hobbies, your favorite recording artist or movie star, and finally you can talk about "what you want to be in the future." When I was called on, I froze. I had no idea what a "hobby" was. When it was explained that it was something I did that made me happy, I couldn't conceive of such a thing. My only goal was supposed to be making the regime happy. And why would anyone care about what "I" wanted to be when I grew up? There was no "I" in North Korea—only "we." This whole exercise made me uncomfortable and upset.

When the teacher saw this, she said, "If that's too hard, then tell us your favorite color." Again, I went blank.

In North Korea, we are usually taught to memorize everything, and most of the time there is only one correct answer to each question. So when the teacher asked for my favorite color, I thought hard to come up with the "right" answer. I had never been taught to use the "critical thinking" part of my brain, the part that makes reasoned judgments about why one thing seems better than another.

The teacher told me, "This isn't so hard. I'll go first: My favorite color is pink. Now what's yours?"

"Pink!" I said, relieved that I was finally given the right answer.

In South Korea, I learned to hate the question "What do you think?" Who cared what I thought? It took me a long time to start thinking for myself and to understand why my own opinions mattered. But after five years of practicing being free, I know now that my favorite color is spring green and my hobby is reading books and watching documentaries. I'm not copying other people's answers anymore.

I believe that my teachers at Hanawon had only the best intentions when they warned us how difficult it would be to compete with students who were born in South Korea. This country's academic achievement is rated number one in the world by the Pearson Global Index, a metric that ranks the United Kingdom in sixth place and the United States in fifteenth. We were told that South Korean kids were so obsessed with education that they studied seven days a week, and crammed their free time with tutoring courses to get ahead of their classmates. By telling us this, the Hanawon staff was trying to make sure our expectations of integrating into the public schools were realistic. But in my case, they were robbing me of hope. I almost felt like giving up before I started.

I never knew freedom could be such a cruel and difficult thing. Until now, I had always thought that being free meant being able to wear jeans and watch whatever movies I wanted without worrying about being arrested. Now I realized that I had to think all the time—and it was exhausting. There were times when I wondered whether, if it wasn't for the constant hunger, I would be better off in North Korea, where all my thinking and all my choices were taken care of for me.

I was tired of being so responsible. In China, I was the breadwinner, the one who kept my mother alive. Now I didn't know how I was supposed to go back to being the child again. When we first arrived at Hanawon, my mother and I shared a room with another woman and her daughter, who was about my age. The mother complained that I was too independent and mature, and said I should act more like a kid. But I didn't know what that meant. Inside I felt a thousand years old.

I hated it when people didn't like me, so I tried to act young for the mothers, and I tried to fit in with the other teenagers. I don't know how well that worked. We saw one another every day and took field trips as a group, but I felt very much alone. The staff took us on a tour through Seoul, showed us the war museum and the Han River, and taught us how to buy a ticket and use the subway. It made me nervous, with all the noise and machines, flashing advertisements, and swarms of people everywhere. I smiled and pretended to pay attention. Outside I was a perfect kid, but inside I was churning.

One day, I was standing around the cafeteria, talking with some North Korean kids my age. One of the boys was gossiping about a teenage girl with an infant.

"You can't trust North Korean girls," said another boy. "They've all been trafficked. This one just couldn't hide it."

"I have no idea what you're talking about!" I told them. "What's this trafficking?"

Whenever the subject of China came up, I brushed it aside like that. My mother and I never talked about the past, even when it was just the two of us. We would look at each other and understand what was unspoken: *The birds and mice could still hear us whisper.* My mother had her own challenges with this strange new world we were about to enter. But she had a better attitude about it than I did. Every day that she didn't have to struggle to survive was a good day for her.

We both tried hard to forget the bad memories and move on. I wanted to erase my old life, but its horror would come back to visit me as soon as I fell asleep. My dreams were all nightmares and they usually had the same theme: water was flowing around me and I needed to escape across the river. Someone was always chasing me, but no matter what, I couldn't get away. Sometimes the nightmares were so bad that I would wake myself up screaming. It took me a few moments to recognize the thick blanket on my bed, to remember I was safe, I had survived, I was out.

But sometimes, even in the middle of the day, I wondered if I was still in North Korea and everything else was just a dream.

I must have pinched myself a thousand times a day. I thought that at any moment I might wake up and find myself in my cold house in Hyesan, alone with my sister, lying on the floor and staring at the moon outside the window, wondering when our mother would come back with food.

Sometimes I pinched myself so hard that I bruised and bled, because I needed to feel pain to know that this life was real. Sometimes I did it just to be sure I could feel anything at all. A numbness lingered inside me, like a cold companion that watched me from a distance, unable to engage in the world.

In North Korea, we don't have words for "depression" or "post-traumatic stress," so I had no idea what those things were or whether I might be suffering because of them. The concept of "counseling" was so foreign to me that when it was offered at Hanawon, I had no idea what they were talking about. Recently I have seen studies that indicate nearly 75 percent of recent North Korean defectors in South Korea have some form of emotional or mental distress. To me, this sounds like a low estimate. All of us at Hanawon were trying to act like normal people, while inside the anguish of our past and the uncertainty of our future was eating us alive.

In the early days of the Republic of Korea, newly arrived defectors from the North were treated like heroes and were usually given big rewards, subsidies, and scholarships. But after the famine of the 1990s, a wave of refugees started pouring into South Korea, straining the resettlement system. In fact, the number of defectors in 2009 was the biggest ever, with 2,914 new arrivals.

And now, in contrast with the mostly male, highly skilled defectors of the past, about 75 percent of the refugees were poor women from the northern provinces—like my mother and me. Over time, the resettlement packages had grown smaller and more restrictive. But they were still a lifeline for us as we adapted to our new home.

On August 26, 2009, Hanawon threw a graduation party for the members of Group 129. My mother and I were issued citizenship papers for the Republic of Korea. I felt a huge relief wash over me. I thought this was the final trial on the road to freedom. But almost as soon as we passed through the gates of Hanawon, I started missing it. I was now in the land of choices, where supermarkets had fifteen brands of rice to choose from, and I was already longing to go back to a place where they told us what to do.

As soon as we settled into our new life, I found out how painful freedom could be.

My mother and I received a resettlement package for housing and other expenses worth approximately $25,234 over the next five years. This seems like a lot of money until you consider that it's about what most South Korean households earn in one year. Defectors have to work hard to catch up with average citizens, and many of them never do. We were told we could get a little more money if we agreed to live outside the crowded capital, so my mother and I took the deal and were sent to a small factory town near Asan, about two hours by rail south of Seoul.

Our apartment was assigned to us and paid for by the government. A bank account was set up for my mother, and we were given a one-time stipend to get us started. But we didn't get it all at once. Some Chinese brokers were known to track down defectors in South Korea to collect money they were owed. And there were South

Korean scam artists who would cheat defectors out of their resettlement money. That happened a lot because newly arrived North Koreans were so innocent of the ways of the world.

In North Korea, there are no written contracts, so at Hanawon they kept telling us that everything in this world happens on paper, and once you sign something you are responsible for it. You can't change your mind. But old habits are hard to break and new ones hard to learn. So the government figured that if our payments were stretched out a bit, at least we couldn't lose everything at once. But if they had seen our living arrangement in Asan, they would have realized my mother and I had little to lose anyway.

Our housing complex was perched on a hill at the edge of town, a short walk from a few small shops and a bus line that took you to more populated places. Rents were very low here, and our building was filled with tenants on government assistance, including the very old and disabled who had no families to care for them, several mentally ill people who should have been in an asylum, and us.

We lived in one room with a small kitchen, a mat on the floor for a bed, and a balcony for storage. The building was crawling with cockroaches, people peed in the elevator and the lobby, and there was a crazy man in the apartment next to ours who screamed at all hours of the day and night. Luckily, our neighbor on the other side was a kindly old lady who gave us a rice bowl and some pretty plates she didn't want anymore. We bought a small refrigerator from a secondhand store. The rest of our furnishings came from a grass and concrete island in the parking lot that tenants had turned into a dump for discarded clothes and household items. My mother and I couldn't believe our luck when we found lamps, cookware, a used mattress, and even a small TV. People were constantly moving in and out, so there were lots of new treasures every week. We decided that these South Koreans threw out more useful things than even the Chinese.

Another great thing about South Korea was the affordable fruit in the shops. In North Korea, oranges and apples were unimaginable luxuries, so here my mother loved buying them and slicing them for us to share. She'd had such a hard time in her life, but she always managed to find something to be grateful for. She could also find humor in most things, including herself. For instance, we were always making mistakes with the unfamiliar products around us, and one time my mother squirted my perfume into her mouth, thinking it was breath spray. When she stopped gagging and cursing me, she burst out laughing. Neither of us could stop until tears ran down our faces.

One night shortly after we arrived in Asan, I woke up to the sound of my mother giggling.

"What is it, *Umma*?" I said. "What's so funny?"

"The refrigerator, Yeonmi-ya!" she said. "I just heard it turn itself on."

Twenty-one

A Hungry Mind

My first goal was to meet some real South Koreans. All the people we'd met so far were other defectors, South Korean agents, and specially trained staff. I was also keen to learn more about computers, so I decided to visit a PC Internet room I had noticed among some shops near the apartments. Unlike Internet cafés, which are open to everyone, these are more like private clubs where you pay a small hourly fee to play games and chat with friends online. I brushed my hair into a ponytail, put on some clean clothes, then walked down the hill.

The PC club was on the second floor, at the top of a grubby concrete stairwell. I thought it was incredibly sophisticated, with its colored lights and shiny rows of computer terminals manned by hypnotized-looking young men.

I gathered my courage and pushed open the glass door. The older man at the reception desk glanced up at me as I walked in.

"I'd like to use this PC . . ." I said.

As soon as he heard my accent, he knew I was not from South Korea.

"We don't allow foreigners in this place," he said.

"Okay, I'm from North Korea, but I'm a South Korean citizen now," I said, utterly shocked. I could feel tears stinging my eyes.

"No, you're a foreigner," he said. "Foreigners are not allowed here!"

I turned and ran down the stairs, and I didn't stop running until I got back to our apartment. I felt gutted.

The next day, all I wanted to do was to lie in bed with a blanket over my head, but my mother said I had to get dressed. It was early September, and the school term had already begun. It was time for me to register for classes.

Even though my test scores placed me at the same level as South Korean eight-year-olds, I was almost twice that age and too big for elementary school. So if I wanted a public education, it had to be at the local middle school. I could have chosen a private alternative school just for defectors, but I wanted to learn to fit into South Korea as soon as possible.

The middle school was a modern brick building hung with colorful banners congratulating the students for their victories in academics and sports. My mother and I met with an administrator in his office, and the first thing he told me was how hard it would be to succeed. "You know, we had a North Korean boy here a few years ago," he said, "but he never could catch up, and he failed." He gave me a meaningful look, as if to send the message that I, too, was a hopeless case.

"And the uniforms are very expensive here," the principal added. "We'll have to get you a used one your mom can fix up for you."

Then I was led away to meet some of my new classmates. All the girls were wearing their smart uniforms, and I was dressed in a hand-me-down outfit given to me by a social worker. I tried to talk to a few kids, but they just looked at me and walked away. Later, I heard some of the girls talking about me, not caring that I could overhear.

"What's that animal-thing doing here?" said one.

"What's wrong with her accent?" said another. "Is she a spy or something?"

At the end of the day, I walked home with my mother and never came back.

After that, I was so afraid of other people that I refused to leave our apartment. If I tried to go outside, I broke into a cold sweat and my heart pounded so hard that I thought I would die. The only time I felt comfortable outdoors was late at night, when nobody else was around. My mother would walk me to a small playground for the few children who lived in the apartment complex. There I would sit on the swings and rock back and forth while my mother told me about her day or sang me some of the old songs.

"You have to be more confident, Yeonmi," she said. "Why are you so terrified when people look at you?"

But there was no way to explain it to her.

After a month of hiding, I realized I had to force myself back out into the world. Even if many South Koreans believed I had no future, even if they thought I was stupid and backward and untrustworthy, I was going to show them. I was going to make it one way or another. And the first step was to get an education.

Before he died, my father told me about his regrets. He always wanted me to study and to bring home good grades. He knew I had wanted to go to university someday and maybe become a doctor like so many of our relatives. But once he was arrested, that dream became impossible. Now I had a way to honor my father's wishes.

So many things I learned at Hanawon didn't make sense at all. But there was one simple phrase I heard over and over that really struck me: "In a democracy, if you work hard, you will be rewarded." I didn't believe it at first. That was not the way things happened in North Korea, where working hard was rewarded only if you had a good *song-bun* and the right connections. But I knew that I could work hard, and it excited me to think that I might be rewarded for my effort. I didn't have a word for "justice" yet, or even understand the concept, but this was an idea that felt right to me. I had to begin working toward my goals immediately; there was not a moment to waste.

In November 2009, I enrolled in the Heavenly Dream School, a Christian boarding school that was exclusively for young North Koreans, in the nearby town of Cheonan. Almost all the special schools for defectors were run by Christians, and there weren't many options available. This school was the closest to my mother.

I had so much catching up to do. My goal was to earn general equivalency diplomas—GEDs—for middle school and high school at the same time other kids my age would be graduating from regular schools, and then go on to college. There were about fifteen teenagers at Heavenly Dream—although the numbers would go up and down—including some girls I had met at Hanawon. But I was not a popular student. I was determined to lose the one thing that gave away my identity as a defector, so when I talked to people, I practiced speaking in a South Korean accent. The girls thought I was strange and aloof. The teachers told me that I wasn't "opening up" enough. I wasn't interested in spending a lot of time reading the Bible and going to church, which was very important to everybody else. All I wanted to do at the Heavenly Dream School was study. I was so thirsty to learn that I couldn't tolerate any distractions. My nickname was "Learning Machine."

Most of the time, I stayed in my room and read on my own. I remembered the old pleasure of reading books in North Korea, only now there was a lot more to read about than the adventures of Kim Il Sung and Kim Jong Il.

Meanwhile, my mother was relieved that I was going to a boarding school, where I would be safe and somebody would feed me. She was planning a trip to China.

As soon as we were released from Hanawon, my mother got in touch with some brokers in China who sent a woman across the border to Hyesan to ask about Eunmi. We wanted to know if she'd been arrested in China and sent back, like so many other women we knew. But nobody had heard from my sister in the two and a half years she'd been missing.

So we spread word through the trafficking networks in China that we were offering a $10,000 reward for any information about Eunmi. At the same time, my mother applied for a South Korean passport. We lived in poverty during our first months in Asan because we were saving all that we could for our search for my sister. As soon as my mother had her passport in hand, she booked a flight to China.

It's hard to imagine the courage it took for my mother to make this trip by herself. She still spoke almost no Chinese and had never traveled in the country without someone to guide her. Even though she now had South Korean citizenship, there was no way to know whether she would be kidnapped and sold again, or even fall into the hands of North Korean agents who would send her back to her death. But she pushed through her fears and boarded a flight to the resort city of Dalian—because it was cheaper—and took a very long bus ride by herself to Shenyang.

She stayed with our friend Myung Ok, our chat-room boss, while she searched for Eunmi. When we were in hiding, we had been too afraid to contact my father's relatives, who lived in the northeast Chinese city of Yanbian. We had been worried that even making phone calls to try to track them down would bring the police to our door. This time my mother located them through the bank where my father's aunt once worked. It was wonderful to reconnect with that part of the family, but we were disappointed to learn that nobody had heard from Eunmi.

After twenty days in China, my mother came home discouraged. We could not find my sister, but we would not give up hope that she would find us someday. Meanwhile, my mother did not come back completely empty-handed. Before we left for the mission in Qingdao, we stored our belongings at a safe place in Shenyang. We didn't want to be carrying anything that could identify us as North Koreans while we made our escape. This included a small packet of family photographs. Those pictures were all we had left of my father and Eunmi and the family we loved and had left behind. And now they were with us in South Korea.

Another good thing came from this trip. In the past, Myung Ok had refused to defect because she was terrified of getting arrested and sent back to be tortured and executed. But my mother told her about how great it was in South Korea and how the government helped us when we arrived. "Look at this!" she said to Myung Ok, waving her passport in her friend's face. "You can get one of these when you go there, and then you can travel anywhere without fear! You'll be free."

Seeing that passport gave Myung Ok the courage to take the risk. My mother and I made some phone calls and arranged a route for her to escape through Thailand. She departed a few months later and finally made it to South Korea.

I didn't stay at the Heavenly Dream School for very long. In fact, as soon as my mother returned from China, at the end of November,

I dropped out and moved back into the apartment. I didn't feel that I was getting enough of what I needed out of the school's curriculum, and I didn't like all the extra religious activities. I didn't like having to pretend to believe more deeply than I did. And the preaching sometimes reminded me of how the pastor in Qingdao had made me feel so dirty and sinful.

Once I was home, all I did was read. I inhaled books like other people breathe oxygen. I didn't just read for knowledge or pleasure; I read to live. I had only $30 a month to spend, and after expenses, I would use everything I had left to buy books. Some were new; some came from a secondhand store. Even if I was hungry, books were more important than food. I didn't know there were public libraries until much later. It seems hard to believe now, but we had so little information about life in South Korea when we first arrived.

I started with Korean translations of children's books, then moved on to picture books about the countries of the world. I bought books about Roman mythology and world history. I read biographies of Abraham Lincoln, Franklin Roosevelt, and Hillary Clinton. I was interested in America, and I particularly loved biographies because they were about people who had to overcome obstacles or prejudices to get ahead. They made me think I could make it when nobody else believed in me, when even I didn't believe in myself.

I crammed twelve years of education into the next eighteen months of my life. I attended a few other special schools to help me get my general equivalency diplomas for middle school and high school. But even then, I studied best on my own. I vowed to myself to read one hundred books a year, and I did.

I read to fill my mind and to block out the bad memories. But I found that as I read more, my thoughts were getting deeper, my vision wider, and my emotions less shallow. The vocabulary in South Korea was so much richer than the one I had known, and when you have more words to describe the world, you increase your ability to think complex thoughts. In North Korea, the regime doesn't want you to think, and they hate subtlety. Everything is either black or white, with no shades of gray. For instance, in North Korea, the only kind of "love" you can describe is for the Leader. We had heard the "love" word used in different ways in smuggled TV shows and movies, but there was no way to apply it in daily life in North Korea—not with your family, friends, husband, or wife. But in South Korea there were so many different ways of expressing love—for your parents, friends, nature, God, animals, and, of course, your lover.

When I was in the NIS center waiting to go to Hanawon, sometimes they brought people from the outside to ask us to fill out surveys and talk to us. One woman told us about love. She said that if you say "I love you" to plants, they grow more healthily. So it was very important to let someone you care about hear that word from you. She encouraged us to say that word to whoever was sitting beside us at the moment. It was a very weird exercise, but that's when I knew there were ways to express love for friends, or even plants or animals. Everything, even basic human emotions, has to be taught.

I was starting to realize that you can't really grow and learn unless you have a language to grow within. I could literally feel my brain coming to life, as if new pathways were firing up in places that had been dark and barren. Reading was teaching me what it meant to be alive, to be human.

I read literary classics like *Catcher in the Rye*, *Lord of the Flies*, and Tolstoy's short stories. I fell in love with Shakespeare. But it was discovering George Orwell's *Animal Farm* that marked a real turning point for me. It was like finding a diamond in a mountain of sand. I felt as if Orwell knew where I was from and what I had been through. The animal farm was really North Korea, and he was describing my life. I saw my family in the animals—my grandmother, mother, fa-

ther, and me, too: I was like one of the "new pigs" with no ideas. Re-
ducing the horror of North Korea into a simple allegory erased its
power over me. It helped set me free.

When I was at Hanawon, defectors who had already made their
way into South Korean society would sometimes visit us to
share their experiences. One of them gave us a simple tip for how to
make friends with South Koreans: learn about the hottest TV shows
and most popular stars so you can talk about them. Even watching
movies and TV became an education for me. I memorized the actors'
names and the storylines of their movies and shows. I wrote down all
the music groups and listened to as many songs as I could so I could
recognize the biggest hits of the seventies, eighties, and nineties.

I read articles about celebrities, learning their scandals and histories so that I could talk about them as if I had lived in South Korea all
my life. I was amazed by all these celebrity weddings and designer
gowns. I had no idea what a designer was, but now there was a room
at school where I could access the Internet and look things up. The
whole idea of a "celebrity" was very strange to me. Beautiful people in
South Korea were adored like our Leader in the North. But the big
difference was that in South Korea, people had a choice of whom to
idolize.

Gradually, my northern accent vanished, and I started to sound
like someone from Seoul. I learned how to dress, eat, and make conversation like a South Korean. If a person who didn't know me asked
where I was from, I just said "Asan," and let them believe whatever
they wanted. I did everything I could to distance myself from my
past. I never contacted anyone who had known me in China. My
mother stayed close to Sun Hi and Myung Ok after they settled in the
South, but not me. I wanted nothing to do with that part of my life,

and already it was beginning to seem unreal to me, like something from a half-remembered dream.

My mother told me it wasn't healthy for me to stay home reading all the time. She urged me to go back to boarding school, so in the spring of 2010, I enrolled at another Christian academy for defectors to earn my middle school GED, then switched to the Seoul campus of the Heavenly Dream School to finish high school. I still avoided going to class and did most of my work on my own. But I was scoring well on my tests.

In April 2011, just two years after my mother and I landed in South Korea, I took my high school GED exam and passed. It was a sweet victory. I thought about all those people who had written me off: the pastor in Qingdao, the agent who interrogated me, the principal who dismissed me, and the many teachers who told me this day would never come. Being told that what I wanted to do was impossible had motivated me, and earning the GED showed me, for the first time, that there could be justice in my life. Hard work would be rewarded.

My mother couldn't believe that the very slow child she raised in Hyesan had earned her high school GED. But she reminded me that in North Korea we say, "You can't tell how smart a child is until he grows up." She was not the kind to say outright that she was proud of me, but I could tell that she was.

My mother went through her own trials, trying to adapt to life in South Korea. She worked very hard at a number of menial jobs that are typically held by newly arrived North Korean defectors. She cleaned and washed dishes in a coffee shop that served food, where she met a man who worked at a local sauna. They started dating, and he got her a job selling snacks at the spa where he worked. Unfortunately, he turned out to be a very violent man. I didn't realize how bad it was until one night while I was at the Dream School in Seoul, I got a phone call from a hospital in Asan.

"It's your mother," said the nurse. "You need to come get her."

I pulled on my clothes and ran to the subway, catching the first morning train to Asan at around five a.m. First, I stopped by our building. When I got there, the hallway was spattered with blood and there was a huge pool of blood in our apartment. Our neighbor told me there had been a terrible fight. My mother's boyfriend had hit her on the head with a heavy metal pan and knocked her out, then run away, leaving her for dead. The neighbors had called the police, who had come and taken her to the hospital.

My poor mother was in sorry shape, all bandaged up and suffering from a bad concussion. When I went home to clean up the blood, she checked herself out of the hospital because we couldn't afford the expense. There was no money for a cab, and a bus would have made her too nauseated, so she walked home by herself. It just broke my heart when she came through the door, so exhausted and dizzy. Even in the South, life was not easy for us.

She never pressed charges against the boyfriend. The police interrogated him and wanted to prosecute, but my kindhearted mother forgave him and asked them to let him go. I think that after her experiences with the North Korean police, she would not put anyone through that kind of torture, even someone who had tried to kill her. She didn't know there was a difference in the way the police worked in South Korea.

After he attacked her, my mother tried to break up with this man, but he stalked her and came to the apartment at all hours to threaten her. After a couple of months, she gave up resisting and got back together with him again. But he was a violent man, and he continued to abuse her. Sometimes I would get a text from her saying, "If I die tonight, you know he did it."

It drove me crazy to think that my mother had endured so much suffering to be free, and now that she was finally in South Korea, she had to live in fear. Once she had refused to press charges, it seemed like the police could do nothing more to protect her.

There had to be a better way. If they couldn't protect her, I thought, then maybe I could. I could learn the law and become a police officer, or even a prosecutor. In North Korea, the police were the ones who took your money and hauled you away to prison. In China, I froze in fear anytime I saw a uniform, because the police there would arrest me on the spot. Police officers had never protected me from anything in my life. But in South Korea, protection was their job description. And so I chose to run toward the thing I feared the most and join their ranks.

I did some research and found that the best place in the country to get a degree in police administration was Dongguk University in Seoul. So that was where I decided to apply for college.

Twenty-two

Now on My
Way to Meet You

D onngguk University is perched on a steep hill in central Seoul, with views on all sides overlooking the city and the wooded slopes of Namsan Park. The college was founded in 1906 by Buddhists and, although it accepts scholars of all faiths, its four principles reflect the school's origins:

> Steady one's clean mind.
> Behave truly and reliably.
> Love people with benevolence.
> Save mankind from agony.

These sounded like tenets I could stand behind, particularly the last one. I had used my first two years of freedom to work on myself, awakening my mind and opening it to the possibilities of the world. I was safe now, but I couldn't stop thinking about my family and friends and all the others who were still suffering, and my sister, who was

still missing. There had to be some reason why I had escaped and survived and found my freedom and they had not. But it was still just a
notion that I couldn't fully express.

My more immediate mission was to get accepted by this presti-
gious university. As a North Korean defector, I had half of my tuition
paid for by the government while the school paid the other half—as
long as I kept up my grades—so cost was not an obstacle. But I knew
my unusual educational background would be an issue, to say the
least. Like all defectors, I was allowed to bypass South Korea's noto-
rious eight-hour-long College Scholastic Ability Test, but I still had to
pass rigorous tests to enter the university, including an oral exam.
Everything rested on the interview I had scheduled with the admissions office in early summer 2011.

I was so nervous about it that I arrived on the campus at five a.m.
I sat on a bench in the cool morning air, waiting for the time of the
interview to arrive. There is a large statue of the Buddha at one end of
the large central quad, and right before my appointment, I stood in
front of it to pray.

Although I had embraced Christianity fully while I was among the
missionaries in China, my beliefs were not confined to any one faith.
I had been raised without any religion except the worship of dictators,
and my spirit was still searching for a place to rest. Despite all evi-
dence to the contrary, I believed in a benevolent power guiding the
universe, a loving force that somehow nudged us in the direction of
good instead of evil. I believed that Jesus was part of that force, along
with the Buddha, and all the spiritual beings that we called on in our
moments of despair and need. My father was there, too. And so as I
stood before the Buddha, I placed my hands together in front of my
heart and spoke to my father, asking him for guidance. I still felt a
strong connection to him, that all I needed was to ask and he would
come to me to give me strength. I felt him strongly that morning.

It was obvious that I was not prepared for college, and the small panel of professors in the interview room knew it. I had to convince them that I was worthy.

"Hello, my name is Yeonmi Park. I was born in Hyesan, North Korea. I came here a short time ago, with almost no education, and I have achieved a great deal in two years. I can guarantee you that if you put your trust in me, I won't let you down."

I shocked myself with my self-confidence. The professors looked surprised, too.

"You have done very well so far," said one of them. "But you have so little formal education and you haven't studied English, which you need to graduate."

Another said, "We all know that a lot of North Koreans don't graduate once they start college. How can you promise me that you will not be a failure, too?"

I looked up at them and said, "Yes, it's true I don't have the same skills as other applicants, but I can learn them. More important, while these students were in school, I was learning from life. And so I have something to offer that they do not. If you give me the chance, I can do this and make you proud of me."

In August, I checked the online admissions notices and learned that I had been accepted at Dongguk University in the criminal justice department.

I put my face in my hands and wept. Finally someone believed in me.

The school year in South Korea begins in early March, so I had seven months before I started at Dongguk. Because I had not yet officially graduated from the Heavenly Dream School in Seoul, I lived in school housing and attended some classes while I prepared myself for college. I also worked part-time as a clerk in a two-dollar store as well as setting places and clearing plates in the wedding hall of a fancy hotel. I don't think I would have been hired if I sounded or looked like a North Korean defector. So I let them think I was from Seoul.

I was ready to forget my past and start fresh with a whole new identity as a South Korean college student. But then I got a call from the producer of a national cable TV show on EBS, the Educational Broadcasting System, toward the end of 2011. He wanted to interview a North Korean defector, and he had heard my name from someone connected with Hanawon. I agreed to meet with him, and I told him the story of my escape across the desert and my search for my sister who had disappeared into China. At the end of our conversation, he told me he was looking for an articulate and ambitious young defector to appear on a segment of his show. Would I be interested?

I felt a panic rising in me and I immediately answered, "No!"

"But it's an important show, and it will be seen everywhere," said the producer. He paused. "And maybe it will help you find your sister."

I hadn't thought of this possibility before. South Korean television was watched online all over China. If I were to tell Eunmi's story on TV, then maybe she would see it and find a way to contact us so we could help her escape.

On the other hand, I would be taking a big risk going public. There were several women other than our friends now living in South Korea who knew me and what I had done to survive in China. My hopes for a career in law or criminal justice might be destroyed if they came forward to expose me.

I discussed the offer with my mother, and we decided that it was worth taking the chance if it meant finding Eunmi.

I spent a couple of days taping the segment. Mostly they filmed me walking around beaches and amusement parks with an older defector while we talked about the generation gap between North Koreans my age, who had access to foreign DVDs, and his generation, who had a different mind-set. At one point, they brought us to an accordion academy run by a couple of North Korean defectors, and they taped me while I listened to them playing accordions and singing songs from the old country. An enormous wave of grief rolled over me, and I couldn't stop myself from crying in front of the camera. I told them how Eunmi used to play the accordion when we were children in Hyesan. And that I hadn't seen her in five years and missed her so much.

After the show aired, in January 2012, I jumped every time my phone buzzed with a strange number, hoping it would be a message from Eunmi in China. But days went by and there was no word from my sister.

I started classes at Dongguk in March 2012. The university was like a huge banquet of knowledge spread out before me, and I couldn't eat fast enough. In my first year, I took courses in English grammar and conversation, criminology, world history, Chinese culture, Korean and American history, sociology, globalization, the Cold War, and more. On my own I read the great Western philosophers, such as Socrates and Nietzsche. Everything was so new to me.

I could finally think about something beyond food and safety, and it made me feel more fully human. I never knew that happiness could come from knowledge. When I was young, my dream was to have one bucket of bread. Now I started to dream great dreams.

Unfortunately, the more practical requirements of college life stopped me short. In my very first class, the professor divided us into teams to create a presentation. As soon as I met with my group, I had to admit that I had no idea what a presentation was or how I could contribute. The others took on the computer and design work, and they assigned me to "research." I wasn't sure what that meant. I was largely self-educated up to this point, and I realized that my academic career was going to be a disaster unless I immediately developed some computer and research skills. So in addition to my course work, I went online to teach myself the basics.

I had rented a tiny basement apartment in a neighborhood near the university, but I never spent much time in my apartment. During the school year, I practically lived in Dongguk's modern, glass-walled library, with its stacks of tantalizing books and its high-speed Internet access. It became my playground, my dining room, and sometimes my bedroom. I liked the library best late at night, when there were fewer students around to distract me. When I needed a break, I took a walk out to a small garden that had a bench overlooking the city. I often bought a small coffee from a vending machine for a few cents and just sat there for a while, staring into the sea of lights that was metropolitan Seoul. Sometimes I wondered how there could be so many lights in this place when, just thirty-five miles north of here, a whole country was shrouded in darkness. Even in the small hours of the morning, the city was alive with flashing signs and blinking transmission towers and busy roadways with headlights traveling along like bright cells pumping through blood vessels. Everything was so connected, and yet so remote. I would wonder: Where is my place out there? Was I a North Korean or a South Korean? Was I neither?

Ironically, one of my most difficult classes was called "Understanding North Korea." For the first time, I learned details about the political and economic system I was born into. I spent a lot of my energy trying to keep my jaw from dropping open in class. I couldn't believe that the public distribution system used to give most people a 700-gram ration of grain *every day* before the famine. When I was a child, we would have been lucky to be able to buy that much food in a week for the whole family! The class taught that Great Leader Kim Il Sung killed or purged as many as 1.6 million people. I was in shock. I still had trouble trusting what I learned, although now some of it made more sense to me than believing that Kim Jong Il could control the weather with his mind.

Although I usually went out of my way to sit in the front of the class, take a lot of notes, and ask my professors for extra help, I never spoke to the instructor of this course. And I never told him that I was from North Korea.

I guessed correctly that almost nobody at Dongguk had seen me on the EBS segment about my life as a defector, and I never volunteered any information about myself. The students in my own department knew my background, but not those outside my major. And I had a lot of friends who didn't know I was North Korean. I might have been able to keep up this make-believe life if I could have let go of my quest to find Eunmi. But that was not possible.

Shortly after the EBS broadcast, I received a phone call from the producer of a new cable TV show called *Now on My Way to Meet You*. She wanted me to make an appearance.

At the time, *Now on My Way* was a talk and talent show that featured a revolving cast of attractive young women who chatted with celebrities, sang, danced, and performed in comedy skits. What made this program different was that all the panelists were North Korean defectors. (It evolved to include men and older women.) The show was created to raise awareness about defectors and challenge the stereotypical image of North Koreans as grim, robotic, boring people. The sketches poked fun at some aspects of life in the Hermit Kingdom and also at the prejudices defectors had to overcome in the South. But it was run by the station's entertainment—not educational—department, and its tone was as light and playful as its colorful, mod soundstage. A lot of the banter was silly, and the interviews were heavily edited, but that was part of its charm.

Now on My Way was quickly developing a huge following among South Koreans, who knew next to nothing about North Korea, and surveys showed that viewers had a more positive attitude about defectors after watching. At the end of many shows, one of the North Korean guests was given time to send a message to a loved one she had left behind. It was always an emotional, tearful segment that brought home the raw heartache beneath the smiles of all the lovely women onstage.

At first I resisted the offer to be on the show. I still held out hope that the EBS program would bring a response from Eunmi. But as the weeks and then months went by, I realized I needed to generate a bigger audience to reach my sister. *Now on My Way* seemed like the perfect choice. I was still worried that someone from my past would recognize me, but I put it out of my mind and moved ahead—which is something I've always been good at.

When I first arrived on the set, I asked them to disguise my real name, thinking it would protect my relatives in North Korea as well as help me keep my privacy.

The producers interviewed me about my life, and I told them how our fortunes had gone up and down, but we had been privileged at one time. I told them how I had seen videos and played Nintendo, how my father had been a party member and I had traveled to Pyongyang. Most of the other women the producers and writers had interviewed—this was only their third show—came from extremely poor families in the northern provinces, so they had heard terrible stories about starvation and suffering. To them, my life sounded super elite, and they needed somebody like that on the show to provide a contrast.

Because I no longer even thought about it, there was no reason for me to go into detail about what had happened to us after my father's arrest, about the months my sister and I were left alone in our freezing house in Hyesan with very little food and no lights to banish the terrifying darkness. I didn't need to mention the times my sister and I roamed through the hills, eating leaves and roasting dragonflies to fill our bellies. Or the bodies we tried not to look at when we walked to school. And certainly not what happened in China.

As they prepared me for the taping, I was transformed into Ye Ju, the privileged North Korean. I shook out my schoolgirl ponytail, put on a dress and high heels, and let the makeup artists turn me into a North Korean Cinderella. I learned the song and dance numbers with ease, and I was happy to chat with celebrities about anything they wanted to hear. I just hoped the sound of my voice would somehow carry all the way to China.

After that first show, the producers invited me back, and I became a regular guest for a while.

Before every taping, the producers and writers would e-mail each cast member with a list of questions about the show's topic. Then, in the studio, we would read through a script that was based on our answers. In one of them, I was called the "Paris Hilton of North Korea." I had to check the Internet to find out who that was. Later, when my mother appeared on the show, they projected some of our family pictures that showed her wearing some fashionable outfits. "It's my mother who really is the Paris Hilton," I said. "My mother even carried Chanel handbags when she lived in North Korea!" Of course, I did not mention that those handbags were secondhand knockoffs from China. Or that our affluent lifestyle did not last for long. But my mother and I were trying to give answers we thought the audience wanted to hear. It was like echoing that pink was my favorite color to please my teacher.

Still, compared with some of the women on the show, we had led privileged lives. Even in our poorest days, we were better off than the street children who begged for crumbs in the train station, who had never used soap or tasted meat. Some of the others in the studio had lived through those nightmares and more. I don't know if it was because I was still in denial about the wickedness of the Kims or about my own identity as a North Korean, but sometimes I thought my "sister" cast members were exaggerating their hardships.

"She thought the others were lying," my mother told one of the show's hosts in a segment that haunts me to this day. "Sometimes Yeonmi calls me after a taping and asks me, 'Am I really a North Korean? I sometimes cannot understand what the other sisters are saying.'"

We were both caught up in our roles. But my mother was being truthful when she said I didn't realize how much other people were suffering. And she was right when she said that being on the show changed me, because I "learned a lot about the reality of North Korea."

Eventually I began to really listen to what the other women were saying. Their stories reinforced what I was learning in college. Like witnesses taking the stand, one by one, my sisters made a case against the heartless regime that treated all of us as if we were trash to be discarded without a thought. Each story awakened more of my own memories and slowly began to fill my heart with purpose. Kim Jong Il, who was supposed to be immortal, had died in 2011, and his pudgy young son, Kim Jong Un, inherited the family dictatorship. The Kims I had once worshipped as gods were now revealed to be criminals. And criminals deserve to be punished.

Unfortunately, being on a hit show in South Korea did nothing to help me find my sister. With tears streaming down my face, I had sent Eunmi a message at the end of one show, begging her to contact us if she could hear my voice, wherever she was. But all that returned to me was silence.

Twenty-three

Amazing Grace

Looking back, it might have been crazy to think I could keep my life as a South Korean college student separate from my identity as a North Korean defector on a hit television show. Because I used a pseudonym and wore a lot of makeup when I taped *Now on My Way to Meet You*, I somehow thought nobody would recognize me. But eventually most of my professors and friends at Dongguk figured out it was me on that show, and some of them were shocked and disappointed that I hadn't told them who I really was. Of course, I still wasn't sure who I was myself, or who I wanted to be. I was sometimes recognized on the street—which usually terrified me until I realized that the stranger was a fan and not a North Korean agent or someone popping up from my past.

Before long, the stress of being a full-time student, working on the show, and tutoring myself online started to wear me down. I was so busy that I rarely slept and often forgot to eat. The criminal justice department at Dongguk required physical and military training as well as academic course work, and when the semester first started, I had to run almost every weekday and exercise all the time. My weight dropped to below eighty pounds, and I was often dizzy. I couldn't take it physically and had to stop the training. But I continued to lose weight, and during final exams I collapsed and ended up in the emergency room. The doctors told me I was suffering from stress and malnutrition. I was literally working myself to death.

Because I had to give up my physical training, my options in law enforcement were probably limited. But I thought I might continue to study the law. The more I learned about justice, the more it appealed to me. However, it was clear that whatever course of study I chose, I would need to learn English, and I wasn't improving fast enough. So during the July and August break, I signed up for the summer program at an English language academy on the tropical island of Cebu in the Philippines.

I had saved my money from appearing on the show, and this trip was the first thing in my life I had ever done just for myself. At first I was reluctant, but some of my friends persuaded me to go. I was so excited to see more of the world and learn at the same time. But because the academy was filled with South Koreans, I didn't get much practice in English. I made a lot of new friends who thought I was also South Korean. I ate a lot of mangos and sat in the shallow waters, watching colorful fish dart around my toes. I still couldn't swim, but sometimes my new friends took me in the deep water piggyback, the way my sister used to do in the Yalu River.

I was starting to wonder if I would ever see her again.

My grades for the first semester at college were posted online. Out of nearly ninety students in my major, I placed thirty-third. It amazed everyone—including me—because criminal justice was the most demanding department in the whole university. My performance continued to improve over the next year, and by the end of the spring semester in 2013, my rank in class was fourteenth. Not only did this prove to the school administrators that a North Korean defector could compete with South Koreans—I proved it to myself. I was finally living a life with no limits.

I n the summer of 2013, I decided to take some time off from both school and the TV show. My mother and I had resigned ourselves to the fact that Eunmi might be missing for a very long time, although we still held out hope that she was alive, somewhere. My mother had started seeing a very kind man with his own contracting business, and her violent ex-boyfriend finally dropped out of our lives. Now that her life was happier and more stable, I felt free to leave home for several months.

I had been reading the biographies of American civil rights heroes like Martin Luther King Jr. and Rosa Parks, and others who had sacrificed their safety and even their lives so that others could be free. I was drawn to their stories, and by the notion that living a meaningful life requires embracing something bigger than yourself. My mother knew this already. She had always told me that to be happy, you must give to others, no matter how poor you are. And she thought that if she had something to give, it would mean that her own life would have some value. Other than the sacrifices I had made for my family, my life to this point had been very selfish. Now, instead of just focusing on my own needs, working every hour of the day to improve myself, maybe I could become someone useful to others.

While I was attending the Seoul Heavenly Dream School, a team from Youth With A Mission, a Christian youth group from Tyler, Texas, came to preach to us. They told me about a five-month volunteer mission to serve the poor, which included twelve weeks of Bible study in Texas. Doing this work seemed like a way to repay some of the great debt that I owed to the missionaries who had sacrificed so much to help me escape to Mongolia. And it was a way to visit America and see some of the world without having much money or knowing much English. I still wasn't a devout Christian, but I was excited to challenge myself working with this young and dedicated group.

I felt a little queasy as the wheels touched down at George Bush Intercontinental Airport in Houston, but this time it wasn't because of motion sickness. I was suddenly in enemy territory. As we filed off the plane, my head was filled with images of big-nosed Yankee soldiers driving bayonets into helpless North Korean mothers. Propaganda from my childhood was still embedded in my brain, and the feelings I was trained to feel could still pop up without warning. What was I doing visiting these evil people? But as soon as I took one look around the airport, all my dread melted away. There were parents holding their children's hands, people eating chips, packs of teenagers wearing team jerseys. The only difference between us was that we spoke a different language. It amazed me how quickly a lie loses its power in the face of truth. Within minutes, something I had believed for many years simply vanished.

I changed planes and flew into Tyler, a small city about a hundred miles southeast of Dallas. The whole airport seemed about the size of a waiting lounge at Incheon, and I thought to myself, *Is this America? I thought it was much bigger.* A South Korean missionary picked me up and drove me through miles of farmland. Then we pulled through the gates at the Youth With A Mission campus, which used to be a cattle ranch, and kept driving. I was starting to realize what a big place America was, after all. It seemed even bigger just an hour or so later when I joined a group of students on a trip to a nearby Walmart Supercenter to buy some food. I thought it was the fanciest store I had ever seen, and I couldn't believe how enormous it was. And all the products were giant, too. I grabbed a huge blue tube of oatmeal with a friendly-looking old grandpa on the box. I had to try some bright orange macaroni and cheese, which I had never seen before and which you could cook in a microwave, so that was very exciting. I bought a bag of tortilla chips that was almost as big as me. And I bought some work clothes and a pair of Adidas that I could never imagine affording before in my life.

So far, America was very impressive.

Back at the ranch, dozens of Bible students from all different states and places all over the world, like Thailand and countries in South America, had gathered for different programs, including my Discipleship Training Program, where we would be "learning about God, learning about the world, learning about ourselves." I spent a lot of time with another young North Korean defector and several South Korean missionaries. So I had lots of people to talk to—unfortunately, not much of it in English. But I practiced it whenever I had a chance to talk to an American. What I discovered was that I really needed to be studying Spanish. After the initial training, about twenty of us were going on a nearly two-month mission to Costa Rica.

We landed in the capital, San José, and then went on by bus to the coastal fishing town of Golfito. Ours was a mercy mission to share the gospel and give physical help to those in need. We ministered to prostitutes and drug addicts, we picked up trash and cleaned shelters and generally did good works. It was the late summer rainy season, and nights were almost as hot as the days. Some of us slept on the balcony of the pastor's house, which was also used as a church on Sundays. We slept on top of sleeping bags that were usually soaking wet, and although we had a mosquito net, I have never had so many insect bites in my life. My legs were swollen and infected, and I was so miserable, I thought about giving up and going home.

But then a remarkable thing happened: Despite my distress, I stopped praying for myself. For the first time in my life, I found my-self praying for others. And then I realized why I was there.

The feeling had been growing in me for some time now. I had read a powerful book called *Don't Beat Someone, Even with Flowers,* written by a famous Korean actress and humanitarian named Kim Hye Ja, who became an ambassador for the World Vision International charity after she was taken on a tour of Ethiopia's famine camps in the 1990s. Her moving account of the misery in Africa, India, and other places opened my eyes. It taught me the meaning of compassion.

Until I read her book, I thought North Koreans were the only ones suffering in the world. And even though many defectors talked openly about starvation and brutality, only a handful of women publicly admitted to being raped or trafficked. And certainly not as children. It was too shameful to discuss. So I thought I was the only one who had gone through these horrible things. But now I read that this had happened to other girls and women around the world. I was not alone. It made me realize that I was too absorbed in my own pain. But I still did not know how to cry for a stranger's suffering. As far as I knew, it was impossible, because no stranger had ever cried for me.

I had chosen Youth With A Mission because I knew they served some of the poorest and most forgotten communities, but I came to understand that I wasn't there for other people—I was there for my-self. These homeless men and women in Costa Rica might have thought I was ladling rice and picking up trash for them—but I was actually doing it for me.

Through helping others, I learned that I had always had compassion in me, although I hadn't known it and couldn't express it. I learned that if I could feel for others, I might also begin to feel compassion for myself. I was beginning to heal.

W hen our time was up in Costa Rica, we flew back to the United States to continue our mission among the homeless in Atlanta, Georgia.

The homeless shelter where we served seemed like a palace to me. The homeless people had beds and laptops to use, and a refrigerator to keep their sodas chilled. They were free to come and go. But they were not happy, and they had no hope. They thought they had nothing to offer. I found it astonishing.

Our group served them hot dogs and cleaned their rooms. When we were done, I was asked to talk to a homeless man who was assigned as my partner. My English was still very rudimentary, so I told my story through gestures and simple words. He understood that I was from a place called North Korea, and that I had made some kind of crazy escape. I acted out being hungry and scared, and being chased by police. When I shivered and crawled and said, "Sand, sand, sand!" he understood that I had made it through the desert. I was surprised that he cried when I was finished with my story. I told him that all I wanted was a chance for freedom, just as he had here in America.

The man's emotional response opened my mind to the power of my own story. It gave me hope for my own life. By simply telling my story, I had something to offer, too.

I learned something else that day: we all have our own deserts. They may not be the same as my desert, but we all have to cross them to find a purpose in life and be free.

. . . .

After our program ended in November, a friend from the mission invited me and a boy from North Korea to spend Thanksgiving with her family in Virginia. Esther Choi was a Korean American whose parents had emigrated from South Korea about thirty years before, I was so honored to be staying with her family and I felt an instant connection with them. Because they lived so far away, Korean Americans lovingly clung to their old culture; they were more like North Koreans than the South Koreans I knew. I noticed they even used an old-fashioned vocabulary that was very familiar to me.

It was my first American Thanksgiving, and I loved the idea of making a holiday out of gratitude. Esther's mother was planning to make a big turkey, along with lots of Korean dishes, including kimchi. I was excited because it had been a long time since I had eaten kimchi, my very favorite food. A few days before the holiday, I was riding in the car with Esther and her mother on a trip to pick some special cabbage in a garden belonging to one of their relatives when my cell phone rang.

It was my mother in South Korea. She was almost hysterical.

"Yeonmi! Your sister! I've found your sister!"

My heart flipped over in my chest. Then I took a breath. We had been tricked before by people in China who claimed to have found her just for the reward money, and our hopes would be dashed again when it turned out to be a hoax.

"*Umma*, what do you mean, you found her?" I said.

"She's here, in South Korea. At the National Intelligence Center. They called me."

I screamed so loud that Esther and her mother thought there was some kind of emergency. My mother and I cried and talked at the same time, neither of us believing this was real but hoping it was. My mother told me she was going to be allowed a special visit to see Eunmi tomorrow at the Center, the same place where we had been held when we first arrived. She would bring her phone and put Eunmi on to talk to me.

I hadn't seen or heard a word from my sister in almost seven years. Suddenly, I had to get back to South Korea as quickly as possible. We drove back to the house so I could change my ticket. I had planned to stay for a few more months, visiting different parts of the United States. Now nothing was more important than getting home.

That night, I couldn't sleep. Thoughts were roaring through my head like a runaway river after a dam break. All the walls I had put up to protect myself from the pain of losing my sister had been shattered, and now I had to feel everything, absolutely everything, good and bad. All I could do was try to hold on for dear life.

The next day, I couldn't eat a bite of food, and I paced through the house for hours until the phone rang and I heard my sister's voice. I was so relieved, but I also struggled with what to say.

"I'll be seeing you soon," I told her, after an awkward minute had gone by.

"Yes, see you soon," she said in a tiny, hushed voice.

I recognized something in that voice, and it broke my heart. It was my father's voice after he was released from the prison camp on medical leave. It was the sound of a captive, a tentative voice belonging to someone afraid of saying the wrong thing, afraid of being punished. It was the sound of my own voice, echoing across the years, reminding me of how far we had to go.

I t took me almost three days in planes and in airport waiting rooms to get home. Normally defectors are kept in isolation until their interrogation period is over, but the kind NIS agents made an exception for me to visit Eunmi to "identify her." They led me to a visiting room, and there she was—my sister I'd thought I would never see again, the same delicate heart-shaped face and tiny hands, alive. Again, there was little we could say. We just held each other's hands and cried. I said a silent prayer to my father, who must have been smiling down on us from somewhere. It was done.

E unmi's story belongs only to her, and she deserves her privacy. What I can tell you is that she never saw any of my television appearances while she was in China. She had no idea that we had escaped from North Korea or that we had been looking for her all this time. It was maddening to learn how physically close we had been to one another at times. As we had suspected, Eunmi and her friend had been hidden in one of the traffickers' houses on the outskirts of Hyesan while my mother and I were searching for her and making our own escape. None of us had known that only a thin wall stood between us on that terrible day. We also compared notes and found out that Eunmi had been living in the same province when my mother and I were working in Shenyang. We were close, and yet a world might as well have separated us. There was so little chance of running into each other when everybody was hiding from the law.

Eventually Eunmi discovered the route to escape through Southeast Asia, and that is how she made it to South Korea on her own. She didn't need us to rescue her after all.

When my sister graduated from Hanawon, she moved in with me in my apartment near Dongguk. She got a part-time job and started studying for her GED, just as I had. Because Eunmi was always a better student than I was, I predicted she would catch up even faster, and she did. She earned her equivalency diploma for middle school in about three months, and for high school in seven more months. But for a long time after she was back with us, my sister seemed trapped and distant, as if there were no room inside her heart for me or my mother. It was something we understood very well, and we both gave her space. In time, Eunmi made room for us all, and more.

Twenty-four

Homecoming

Koreans like the New Year so much, we celebrate it twice, first with Western-style parties and fireworks at midnight to mark the beginning of the calendar year, and again, with even more fireworks and festivities, during the three-day Lunar New Year in late January or February. It's the season when we gather with our families and think about the past and make resolutions for the future. After my mother and I escaped from North Korea in 2007, we stopped celebrating the holidays because they made us sad. But the New Year in 2014 wasn't sad at all. Eunmi was safe. And I was full of plans.

First, I wanted to get back to school and finish my degree. I had chosen my major specifically to join the national police agency in order to protect my mother from her violent boyfriend. But as my mind opened up in college, so did my sense of justice, and now I expected to study law. But I didn't expect that within a year I would become an advocate for North Koreans who had no voice and no hope—the kind of person I had once been. Or that I would be stepping into the international arena to speak out for global justice. Or that the North Korean regime would denounce me as a "human rights puppet." And I never thought that I would reveal what had happened to me in China. But I would soon discover that to be completely free, I had to confront the truth of my past.

M y year of reckoning began quietly enough, with a New Year's resolution to learn better English. Even after spending months among the missionaries, I still couldn't hold up my end of a conversation. So I enrolled in an intensive tutoring program in Seoul that matched North Korean defectors with expatriate volunteers. Instead of just one teacher, I signed up with ten of them all at once. My tutors had me reading everything from Shakespeare to the American abolitionist and escaped slave Frederick Douglass. His defiant letter to his former master made me wonder what kind of letter I might write to Kim Jong Un if I had the nerve. Maybe, like Douglass, I would tell him that I was a human being and he didn't own me anymore. Now I owned myself.

When I wasn't reading or studying with my tutors, I listened to English audiobooks and TED talks—even in my sleep. I downloaded all ten seasons of the American TV comedy *Friends*. Ask me anything about Ross and Rachel, and I can tell you. The only drawback, as far as my tutors were concerned, was that I was developing an American accent and speaking in 1980s slang.

My English was greatly improved when I began the new term at Dongguk in March 2014, and I was on track to earn my degree in police administration. I was still occasionally taping episodes of *Now on My Way to Meet You*, but after Eunmi escaped from China, I had less incentive to appear on the show. Instead, I had found another, more direct way to advocate for justice for North Koreans.

In mid-February 2014, I was invited to give a speech about North Korea—in English—to students and faculty at the Canadian Maple International School in Seoul. The head of my tutoring program said it would help me build confidence in my language skills. I wasn't so sure, but I thought—*why not?*

I pulled back my hair and wore a serious navy blue dress for my first real speech. I told the students a little bit about my life, the brainwashing, the lack of freedom, the fear and the starvation. I told them how I was part of a new generation of North Koreans, a black market or *Jangmadang* Generation, who grew up after the old economic system had died with Kim Il Sung. Young people my age were slowly bringing change from within the country, I said. Maybe not much change, but enough to give me hope for my friends and relatives and the millions of others I left behind when I escaped.

Afterward, I answered questions for an hour. One of the students told me that my story had "inspired" him. I had to quickly look the word up with my cell phone. Until then, I didn't know that a story could "inspire" someone, but apparently it did.

Until early 2014, most people—including South Koreans— knew North Korea only through its crazy threats of nuclear destruction and its weird, scary leaders with bad haircuts. But in February, the United Nations released a report documenting human rights abuses in North Korea, including extermination, rape, and deliberate starvation. For the first time, North Korean leaders were being threatened with prosecution in the International Criminal Court for crimes against humanity. But most of the three hundred or so witnesses who contributed to the report remained anonymous, while others had trouble communicating their stories. Suddenly de-

fectors with English skills were needed to give a voice to the millions
of North Koreans trapped behind a wall of silence and oppression.

My speech at the Canadian school led to other invitations to speak,
which led to more speeches and media interviews from Australia to
the United States. In May I coauthored an op-ed piece in *The Washington Post* with Casey Lartigue Jr. Until that spring, I wasn't sure what a
human rights activist was. Now suddenly people were telling me I was
becoming the face of this issue. I knew I wasn't yet qualified to be a
spokesperson for anyone, let alone the North Korean people. But
from that point on, my life took off like a running train. I could not
jump off if I tried. Maybe I thought if I moved fast enough, my past
could not catch up with me.

In June, I flew to Los Angeles for a conference and had to turn
around and fly back to Seoul the next day for my final exams. I never
even got to visit Hollywood on that trip, although I was hoping to run
into Leonardo DiCaprio to tell him how much *Titanic* had meant to
me growing up in North Korea.

It was around this time that I received a call from a South Korean
police detective who had been assigned to monitor my mother and
me. All defectors are paired with a police officer for five years after
their arrival in South Korea to help them resettle safely. My detective
usually just wanted to know my schedule and see how I was doing. But
this time was different. He said he had been instructed to check on
my safety, because word had come down that I was being watched
closely by the North Korean government. He didn't tell me how he
got this information, only that I should be careful what I said. It could
be dangerous.

If this was supposed to scare me, it worked. It had never occurred
to me that the regime would think I was important enough to be a
threat. Or to threaten me. The detective had spoken to my mother

and frightened her, too. She wanted me to stop all this crazy activism right away. Why couldn't I just live a normal life and finish my education before trying to save the world? But the more I thought about it, the angrier I got. I had risked my life to escape from North Korea, yet they were still trying to control me. I would never be free if I let them do that.

My grades for the spring semester at Dongguk remained above average, and I had every intention of finishing the school year. I returned to college for a few weeks in September 2014, but again my life was overtaking my best-laid plans.

I had accepted a number of invitations in Europe that October, including one to represent North Korea at the annual One Young World Summit in Dublin, Ireland. It was like a United Nations for youth leaders. I was to be introduced by James Chau, a British journalist and humanitarian who is famous throughout Asia as the anchor of China Central Television. In preparation, we spent an emotional morning talking about our lives, and I told him some of the details of my story. For the first time I planned to deliver a speech about the horrors of human trafficking in China—although I had no intention of revealing that I, too, had been trafficked.

We were told to wear the traditional costume of our home country, so I was dressed in a flowing pink and white *hanbok* when I took the stage to give my short speech in front of all 1,300 delegates, guests, and media representatives at the conference.

Before James began his introduction, I was nervous about what I was going to say. I was sitting on a stage with young activists from places like Ukraine and South Africa, and I was afraid I wouldn't be a strong enough speaker to represent my people at this forum. I distracted myself by trying to concentrate on how to properly pronounce the words "international" and "execution" in my prepared speech. But when James began to tell my story, tears started running down his face. I reached out to comfort him, but that made him weep even more. By the time he had described how my mother sacrificed herself to be raped, and how I buried my father's ashes on a lonely mountain in China, I was crying with him.

One of my great fears has always been losing control of my emotions. Sometimes I feel an anger like a dense ball inside me, and I know if I ever let it out, it might explode and I won't be able to contain it. I worry that when I start to cry, I may never be able to stop. So I always have to keep these feelings deep down inside me. People who meet me think I'm the most upbeat and positive person they have ever met. My wounds are well hidden. But that day in Dublin, they were there on the stage for all to see. As I walked to the podium with my prepared speech rolled up in my hand, I fought to speak through my tears.

The audience was already on its feet, and I could see that everybody in the room was crying with me as I struggled to steady myself.

I abandoned my opening statement and attempted to say that I was here to speak for my people, not for myself. But I instantly lost my command of English and had to take a deep breath and start again.

"North Korea is an unimaginable country . . ." I began. I told the people in the room that in North Korea you could be executed for making an illegal international phone call. I told them how, when I was a child, my mother told me not to whisper because even the birds and mice could hear me.

"The day I escaped North Korea, I saw my mother raped by a Chinese broker who had targeted me," I said, letting the tears flow down my face. I told them how North Korean refugees were vulnerable in

China. "Seventy percent of North Korean women and teenage girls are being victimized. Sometimes sold for as little as two hundred dollars . . ."

I had opened a door and stepped outside into the light of day. I didn't know where this path would take me, but I could see that I was not alone.

"When I was crossing the Gobi Desert, I wasn't really afraid of dying as much as I was afraid of being forgotten. I was scared that I would die in the desert and nobody would know, nobody would know my name or would care if I had lived or died. But you have listened. You have cared."

Everybody in the audience was back on their feet, crying with me. I looked around and knew that justice was alive in that room. I felt, at least for that moment, that there was hope for all of us.

But there was still one more desert for me to cross.

After my speech, I managed to get through the rest of the program before I retreated to my hotel room and collapsed. When I finally checked my phone, my mailbox was brimming with requests for interviews from media all over the world. What followed was a whirlwind—but I was oddly detached from it all, as if a mechanism for survival had kicked in and removed me to a safe emotional distance. Part of me was watching the other half make the rest of my appearances.

I gave dozens of interviews during my three weeks in Europe. I lost track after a while. I even agreed to be filmed by the BBC outside the North Korean embassy in London, which filled me with such cold, black terror that I could barely speak. I never used a translator, never thought that the journalists might not understand what I was saying or that I might not understand their questions very well. I also believed that by changing a few details about my family's escape to China, I could continue to hide the fact that I had been trafficked. I thought that if I was truthful about everything else, then it was okay; if what I lived through was real, then the details shouldn't matter. Mostly I was reacting, improvising like a jazz musician playing the same melody a little differently each time, unaware that there might be people out there keeping score.

L ess than a month after my speech in Dublin, I began working on this memoir. It's an odd thing for someone who has just turned twenty-one to be writing the story of her life, especially someone with a secret she has been trying to hide for years. But as soon as I began writing my memories down, I knew that I could no longer hold anything back. How could I ask people to face the truth about North Korea, to face the truth about what happens to the women who escape into China and fall into the hands of brokers and rapists, if I couldn't face it myself?

After I returned to Seoul in November, my mother and sister and I stayed up one whole night, talking about what to do. There were things that happened in China that my mother and I had never told Eunmi. We had never even discussed them ourselves. Now the whole world would know the story. Would it be worth it to come forward? I was sure nobody would ever look at me the same way if they knew what had happened to me, and what I had done to survive. For all its bullet trains and modern architecture and K-pop styles, South Korea is still a very conservative country with old-fashioned notions of female virtue. I couldn't imagine a place for me here when my story came out. And what difference would it make? Would anyone listen? Would anyone care enough to try to change things?

My mother and sister and I talked and cried all night. My mother, who once had hoped I would come to my senses and drop my activism, had gone through her own transformation. Now she recognized the potential impact of our story.

"You have to tell the world that North Korea is like one big prison camp," she said. She wanted people to know why we had to escape, and what happened to North Korean women who were sold in China. "If you don't speak up for them, Yeonmi-ya, who will?" she said. My sister agreed.

In the morning, I made my decision. I would write my story fully and completely, holding nothing back about my own trafficking. If my life was to mean anything, it was my only choice.

As soon as I decided to tell my secret, I felt free for the first time ever. It was like a heavy sky had been pushing down on me, pinning me to the earth, and now it was lifted and I could breathe again.

A few months after I began work on the book, I opened my laptop and followed a link to a YouTube video created by one of North Korea's propaganda units. As two newsreaders from the state-run television network spoke to the camera, a large photograph of my face appeared on the screen. Ominous music built in the background, like the soundtrack to a horror movie, while the words came into focus: "The Poisonous Mushroom That Grew from a Pile of Garbage." North Korean media is ridiculed in the West for its outrageous lies and threats, and this insult might even have seemed funny—except that it was deadly serious and aimed at me and my family.

My detective was right about at least one thing—the North Korean government had been watching me. In early 2015, the regime uploaded two separate videos calling me a liar and a "human rights propaganda puppet."

They had sifted through my interviews and attacked me for supposed inconsistencies in my quotes. When the regime couldn't dispute what I said, they invented lies about me and my family. They accused my mother of being immoral, and my father of being a human trafficker because he had helped our neighbors escape to China. For some bizarre reason, they tried to prove that I had lied about my father's death, and they produced a doctor to say he had died of cancer in a hospital in North Korea, not in China.

Worst of all, they paraded my relatives and former friends to denounce me and my family. I hadn't seen Uncle Park Jin, my aunts, and my cousins in eight long years, and it was horrifying to watch them being interviewed on camera. The regime propagandists even tracked down Jong Ae, our kind neighbor in Hyesan, who had helped me and my sister when we were alone and desperate. It was painful to hear them all say bad things about us, but at least I knew they were alive.

I spent the early months of 2015 visiting New York City, where I was invited to audit a class at Barnard College—I still plan to get my degree someday—and learning everything I could about human rights. One afternoon, I was speed-scrolling through the hundreds of friend requests that had piled up on my public Facebook page when a familiar smile flew by. I backpedaled like a cartoon character spinning away from the edge of a cliff . . . and there she was, Yong Ja! It was my best friend from my childhood in Hyesan. I hadn't heard from her since the day I left for China.

"Is this the Yeonmi Park that I know?" the Facebook message began. My hands were trembling so much I could barely see the screen. *Yes! That's me!* I messaged her right away, and she sent me a number to call. She had escaped to China and, like Eunmi, had made her way through Southeast Asia to South Korea. She found out I was alive and in South Korea while she was being interrogated at the National Intelligence Center, and later she was able to track me down through social media. It was so wonderful to hear her voice again. We immediately picked up our friendship, and now we talk all the time online.

I keep hoping that more friends from North Korea will find their way to freedom. My mother had always loved Chun Guen, the boy who wanted to marry me in Hyesan, and she even tried to trace him to help him if he wanted to escape. But we heard a very sad story instead. Less than a year after we left North Korea, Chun Guen's whole family disappeared. The story going around Hyesan was that his father, an agricultural expert, had been blamed by the regime for a disappointing harvest and had been sent to one of the brutal political prison camps. Chun Guen and his mother were sent into internal exile in a small town deep inside one of the northern provinces.

Chun Guen had promised me that he would wait for eight years, and then he would find me. As I write these words, eight years have passed. I wonder where he is, if he is still alive, if he remembers me at all. Although I have moved on with my life, I hope that he makes it to South Korea someday. Like the 25 million others I left behind, Chun Guen deserves to be free.

I n the spring of 2015, my mother returned to China with her partner to recover my father's remains.

After hours of searching the hills above Yangshanzhen, they found the spot where I had carried my father's ashes in the middle of the night, eight years ago. Someone had been tending my father's grave and had even planted a tree that, for years, had stood next to him like a sentinel. Hongwei had kept his promise.

My mother brought my father's ashes back with her to South Korea. We're finally together again as a family. I hope someday to honor my father's final request to bring him back to Hyesan, where he can be buried next to his father and grandfather on the hill overlooking the Yalu River. If that time comes, I will visit my grandmother's grave as well and tell her that, once again, Chosun is whole.

Acknowledgments

Maryanne Vollers, without you, this book would not be possible. You showed me not only your intelligence and grace, but a deep and genuine love for the North Korean people and all humanity. It was a great honor and privilege to work with you and to call you my friend.

I am deeply grateful to the amazing publishing team at Penguin Books: in the UK at Fig Tree, Juliet Annan and Anna Ridley; in the United States at Penguin Press, Ann Godoff and Sarah Hutson.

Special thanks to Karolina Sutton, Amanda Urban, Matthew J. Hiltzik, and Carlton Sedgeley.

Thor Halvorssen Mendoza, you are the big brother I found in this new world. You are the best example of how to stand up for justice and fight against tyranny everywhere. Thank you so much for being my mentor and for teaching me all those interesting new words. My admiration for you is endless.

Thanks to the Human Rights Foundation staff members Alex Gladstein, Sarah Wasserman, Ben Paluba, and John Lechner.

To my friends and mentors at Liberty in North Korea, Hannah Song, Sokeel J. Park, Justin Wheeler, Blaine Vess, Kira Wheeler, Tony Sasso: When I needed you most, you all helped me understand this new world, and you taught me what it means to be a spokesperson for the North Korean people. All the advice you gave me helped me grow into a better person and become a better advocate for freedom.

Thanks to Casey Lartigue Jr. for all his encouragement and support from the very beginning, and to all my English tutors who rocked my world.

Thanks to Jang Jin Sung, my friend and mentor, who helped me understand and survive life on the other side of darkness. Thank you Henry Song, Shirley Lee, and my family of North Korean defectors and freedom fighters who offer me inspiration and friendship: Joseph Kim, Seong Ho Ji, Park Sang Hak, Jihyun Park, and so many others.

James Chau, thank you so much for crying with me for my people. Your encouragement meant everything to me at a difficult time. Without your support and belief, I would never be who I am today.

Joshua Bedell: Your generosity and kindness are immeasurable. Thank you so much for teaching me and guiding me with great patience.

My English family: Charlotte, Adam, Clemency, Madison, and Lucien Calkin, and my good friend Jai J. Smith. Thanks to Bill Campbell and the rest of my Montana family.

My good friends Alexander Lloyd, Cameron Colby Thomson, Daniel Pincus, Jonathan Cain, Daniel Barcay, Gayle Karen Young, Sam Potolicchio, Dylan Kaplan, Sam Corcos, Parker Liautaud, Axel Halvorssen, Uri Lopatin, Peter Prosol, Masih Alinejad, Tommy Sungmin Choi, Matthew Jun Suk Ha, Wolf von Laer, Ola Ahlvarsson, Ken Schoolland, Jennifer Victoria Fong Chearvanont, Malibongwe Xaba, and Li Schoolland.

One Young World: Kate Robertson, David Johns, Ella Robertson, Melanie York, Mathew Belshaw, and all the OYW ambassadors. I'm so honored that you have made me a part of your wonderful community. Your support and deep caring for the North Korean people gives me enormous hope and courage to stand up against tyranny everywhere. Your hard work makes this world a better place every day.

From Women in the World: Tina Brown, Karen Compton, and all the women who inspired me at the conference to be brave and fight for justice, freedom, and equality.

From Renaissance Weekend: Philip Lader, Linda LeSourd Lader, Dustin Farivar, Eric O'Neill, Christine Mikolajuk, Kerry Halferty Hardy, Frank Kilpatrick, Linda Hendricks Kilpatrick, Yan Wang, Justin Dski, Ben Nelson, Mark A. Herschberg, Katherine Khor, Stephanie A. Yoshida, and Janice S. Lintz.

Thanks to the producers and staff at *Now on My Way to Meet You*. And also my professors at Dongguk University, my friends in police administration who helped and encouraged me when I was having a difficult time, and all the refugee schoolteachers and volunteers.

Special thanks to Judd Weiss, Suleiman Bakhit, Todd Huffman, Katy Pelton, Barnard College president Debora Spar, Dean Jennifer G. Fondiller, Sue Mi Terry, David Hawk, Greg Scarlatiou, Curtis Castrapel, Beowulf Sheehan, Esther Choi and her loving family, Christian Thurston, Daniel Moroz, Cat Cleveland, Eunkoo Lee, Ryung Suh, Justice Suh, Madison Suh, Diane Rhim, Joshua Stanton, Sunhee Kim, Jieun Baek, Felicity Sachiko, Paul Lindley from Ella's Kitchen, CJ Adams from Google Idea, Austin Wright, John Fund, Mary Kissel, and Michael Lai from Minerva Schools KGI.

There are a few people whose names I have changed out of respect for their privacy and concern for their safety, including my dear friend "Yong Ja," to whom I give my love and thanks. Thanks also to the missionaries in China, the South Korean pastor, and all those whose names could not appear in this book but are written in my heart.

Keum Sook Byeon, my mother: To be your child has been the greatest blessing and honor in my life. Without your love and sacrifice, I would not exist today. We crossed the icy river and the frozen desert together, and you are the only person who knows me so well that I don't need words to express my feelings. You were the reason for me to live when I was a captive, and you are the reason for me to live in freedom. You inspire me and give me strength to fight for change in our home country.

Eunmi Park, my sister: You are my everything, the greatest miracle and joy I have known. I am so grateful for your giant heart, for all the sacrifices you made for me when we were children, and for how you protected me and comforted me during those long months when we had only each other. You were a mother to me and a best friend. Big sister, thank you so much for coming back to us after seven long years and bringing us happiness again. I am so proud of you. You are my light, and I love you more than life itself.

Park Jin Sik, my father: You are my hero, and I wish you could be here with me to enjoy this freedom. But you are with me all the time, and so I don't need to say anything here except that I love you and miss you so much.

Woo Yang Mang, my mother's partner, and Lee Hong-ki, my sister's wonderful boyfriend: Thank you, both, for bringing such blessings to our family.

For all my relatives who are still in North Korea and suffering from oppression: I feel extremely guilty to put you all in danger, but I hope that someday you will all understand why I had to speak up. I promise that I will work tirelessly to end the injustice you experience every day. I hope the day comes when I can freely visit my homeland and see you all again.

For all the supporters around the world who send me encouraging and touching messages through social media: I could never acknowledge you all in this small space, but you know who you are. Every smile, every small gesture, every tear you shed with me gave me the courage to share a story that I never thought I would share with anyone. Thank you for believing in me. There were times when I had lost my faith in humanity, but you have heard me. You have cared. And this is how, together, we begin to change the world.